Nothing can stop the man with the right mental attitude from achieving his goal; nothing on earth can help the man with the wrong mental attitude.

Thomas Jefferson

People may hear your words, but they feel your attitude.

John C. Maxwell

Attitude is a little thing that makes a big difference.

Winston Churchill

Develop an attitude of gratitude, and give thanks for everything that happens to you, knowing that every step forward is a step toward achieving something bigger and better than your current situation.

Brian Tracy

Ability is what you're capable of doing. Motivation determines what you do. Attitude determines how well you do it.

Lou Holtz

My attitude is that if you push me towards something that you think is a weakness, then I will turn that perceived weakness into a strength.

Michael Jordan

Some people say I have attitude - maybe I do... but I think you have to. You have to believe in yourself when no one else does - that makes you a winner right there.

Venus Williams

Weakness of attitude becomes weakness of character.

Albert Einstein

A positive attitude causes a chain reaction of positive thoughts, events and outcomes. It is a catalyst and it sparks extraordinary results.

Wade Boggs

Our attitude towards others determines their attitude towards us.

Earl Nightingale

You cannot control what happens to you, but you can control your attitude toward what happens to you, and in that, you will be mastering change rather than allowing it to master you.

Brian Tracy

Your attitude, not your aptitude, will determine your altitude.

Zig Ziglar

The greatest day in your life and mine is when we take total responsibility for our attitudes. That's the day we truly grow up.

John C. Maxwell

Excellence is not a skill. It is an attitude.

Ralph Marston

Adopting the right attitude can convert a negative stress into a positive one.

Hans Selye

Everything can be taken from a man but one thing: the last of human freedoms - to choose one's attitude in any given set of circumstances, to choose one's own way.

Viktor E. Frankl

Our environment, the world in which we live and work, is a mirror of our attitudes and expectations.

Earl Nightingale

If you are going to achieve excellence in big things, you develop the habit in little matters. Excellence is not an exception, it is a prevailing attitude.

Colin Powell

I hope the millions of people I've touched have the optimism and desire to share their goals and hard work and persevere with a positive attitude.

Michael Jordan

We cannot change our past. We can not change the fact that people act in a certain way. We can not change the inevitable. The only thing we can do is play on the one string we have, and that is our attitude.

Charles R. Swindoll

For success, attitude is equally as important as ability.

Walter Scott

Choosing to be positive and having a grateful attitude is going to determine how you're going to live your life.

Joel Osteen

Your living is determined not so much by what life brings to you as by the attitude you bring to life; not so much by what happens to you as by the way your mind looks at what happens.

Khalil Gibran

Keep a good attitude and do the right thing even when it's hard. When you do that you are passing the test. And God promises you your marked moments are on their way.

Joel Osteen

Take the attitude of a student, never be too big to ask questions, never know too much to learn something new.

Og Mandino

Watch your manner of speech if you wish to develop a peaceful state of mind. Start each day by affirming peaceful, contented and happy attitudes and your days will tend to be pleasant and successful.

Norman Vincent Peale

Pink isn't just a color, it's an attitude!

Miley Cyrus

Our lives are not determined by what happens to us but how we react to what happens, not by what life brings us but the attitude we bring to life.

Wade Boggs

It is our attitude at the beginning of a difficult task which, more than anything else, will affect its successful outcome.

William James

I think it's my adventure, my trip, my journey, and I guess my attitude is, let the chips fall where they may.

Leonard Nimoy

Civilization is a method of living, an attitude of equal respect for all men.

Jane Addams

Morality is simply the attitude we adopt towards people whom we personally dislike.

Oscar Wilde

Whenever you're in conflict with someone, there is one factor that can make the difference between damaging your relationship and deepening it. That factor is attitude.

William James

The greatest discovery of my generation is that a human being can alter his life by altering his attitudes.

William James

The last of human freedoms - the ability to chose one's attitude in a given set of circumstances.

Viktor E. Frankl

But the attitude of faith is to let go, and become open to truth, whatever it might turn out to be.

Alan Watts

The meaning of things lies not in the things themselves, but in our attitude towards them.

Antoine de Saint-Exupery

Character is the result of two things: mental attitude and the way we spend our time.

Elbert Hubbard

A positive attitude can really make dreams come true - it did for me.

David Bailey

Cock your hat - angles are attitudes.

Frank Sinatra

Having a positive mental attitude is asking how something can be done rather than saying it can't be done.

Bo Bennett

I think whether you're having setbacks or not, the role of a leader is to always display a winning attitude.

Colin Powell

My general attitude to life is to enjoy every minute of every day. I never do anything with a feeling of, 'Oh God, I've got to do this today.'

Richard Branson

There is little difference in people, but that little difference makes a big difference. The little difference is attitude. The big difference is whether it is positive or negative.

W. Clement Stone

As the time goes by, you change, your learn new things, your attitude is different. For the moment, I'm still enjoying ski racing so much that it would be difficult for me to think about ending my career.

Hermann Maier

Our attitudes control our lives. Attitudes are a secret power working twenty-four hours a day, for good or bad. It is of paramount importance that we know how to harness and control this great force.

Irving Berlin

The remarkable thing is, we have a choice everyday regarding the attitude we will embrace for that day.

Charles R. Swindoll

The ideal attitude is to be physically loose and mentally tight.

Arthur Ashe

My attitude is, if someone's going to criticize me, tell me to my face.

Simon Cowell

Attitude determines the altitude of life.

Edwin Louis Cole

You cannot tailor-make the situations in life but you can tailor-make the attitudes to fit those situations.

Zig Ziglar

It is not the body's posture, but the heart's attitude that counts when we pray.

Billy Graham

Our attitude toward life determines life's attitude towards us.

John N. Mitchell

When a woman puts on a heel, she has a different posture, a different attitude. She really stands up and has a consciousness of her body.

Christian Louboutin

The attitude is very important. Because, your behavior radiates how you feel.

Lou Ferrigno

Bad attitudes will ruin your team.

Terry Bradshaw

Attitude is everything.

Diane von Furstenberg

When you ain't got no money, you gotta get an attitude.

Richard Pryor

Time plays a role in almost every decision. And some decisions define your attitude about time.

John Cale

Eagles come in all shapes and sizes, but you will recognize them chiefly by their attitudes.

E. F. Schumacher

I'm only going to stand before God and give an account for my life, not for somebody else's life. If I have a bad attitude, then I need to say there's no point in me blaming you for what's wrong in my life.

Joyce Meyer

A complainer is like a Death Eater because there's a suction of negative energy. You can catch a great attitude from great people.

Barbara Corcoran

Great effort springs naturally from great attitude.

Pat Riley

The reactionary is always willing to take a progressive attitude on any issue that is dead.

Theodore Roosevelt

Really you just gotta keep chugging along and keep a positive attitude and get through all the problems. You gotta face them, otherwise you don't get through.

Lesley Gore

The greatest discovery of my generation is that man can alter his life simply by altering his attitude of mind.

James Truslow Adams

Acting is magical. Change your look and your attitude, and you can be anyone.

Alicia Witt

Most of us start out with a positive attitude and a plan to do our best.

Marilu Henner

The key to life is your attitude. Whether you're single or married or have kids or don't have kids, it's how you look at your life, what you make of it. It's about making the best of your life wherever you are in life.

Candace Bushnell

Happiness is an attitude of mind, born of the simple determination to be happy under all outward circumstances.

J. Donald Walters

You know what's funny to me? Attitude.

Don Rickles

I always spend time exploring the customs and attitudes of the countries I'm using for locations, and interviewing the people who live there. I've visited over 90 countries thus far.

Sidney Sheldon

Individuals need to be willing to face truth about their attitudes, behaviors, even what we want out of life.

Joyce Meyer

A positive attitude is not going to save you. What it's going to do is, everyday, between now and the day you die, whether that's a short time from now or a long time from now, that every day, you're going to actually live.

Elizabeth Edwards

How do you nurture a positive attitude when all the statistics say you're a dead man? You go to work.

Patrick Swayze

Attitudes are more important than facts.

George MacDonald

Good humor is one of the best articles of dress one can wear in society.

William Makepeace Thackeray

When you are thwarted, it is your own attitude that is out of order.

Meister Eckhart

My attitudes have changed, but somebody would have to read all my books to find out how they have.

Irwin Shaw

China and the U.S. are two societies with very different attitudes towards opinion and criticism. In China, I am constantly under surveillance. Even my slightest, most innocuous move can - and often is - censored by Chinese authorities.

Ai Weiwei

There are no menial jobs, only menial attitudes.

William J. Brennan, Jr.

Our future cannot depend on the government alone. The ultimate solutions lie in the attitudes and the actions of the American people.

Joe Biden

Abhorrence of apartheid is a moral attitude, not a policy.

Edward Heath

When you pray for anyone you tend to modify your personal attitude toward him.

Norman Vincent Peale

Stop this attitude that older people ain't any good anymore! We're as good as we ever were - if we ever were any good.

Dolly Parton

Surfers have the most attitude.

Shaun White

Coaches will eventually notice a great attitude, and they respect that.

Heather O'Reilly

I was always the guy getting kicked out of my classes at school for having an attitude problem.

Chevy Chase

The biggest challenge is how to affect public attitudes and make people care.

Jim Fowler

Every baseball crowd, like every theatre audience, has its own distinctive attitude and atmosphere.

Bill Veeck

I am shocked by the easy attitude of many in the media towards disclosing our Nation's secrets.

Todd Tiahrt

I have a Woody Allen Jewish attitude to life: that it's all going to be disastrous. That it hasn't all been that way is simply down to some random quirk of fate.

Antony Sher

It is one of the most effective attitudes of the neurotic to measure thumbs down, so to speak, a real person by an ideal, since in doing so he can depreciate him as much as he wishes.

Alfred Adler

Punk was defined by an attitude rather than a musical style.

David Byrne

Funny is an attitude.

Flip Wilson

If you get a diagnosis, get on a therapy, keep a good attitude and keep your sense of humor.

Teri Garr

With my talent, I can make people laugh and give them another attitude about life. What a blessing that is for me.

Doris Roberts

I've always had a 'Work hard, play hard' attitude to life - I still do - but sometimes you get involved in something that needs a calm, methodical approach.

Damian Lewis

But Jesus changes your attitude towards yourself and towards other people.

Cliff Richard

If you're looking for can-do, earthy-crunchy attitude then you've got to go to Wisconsin.

Dar Williams

There's a certain elitism that has crept into the attitudes of some in journalism, and it played out perfectly over the issue of these little American flag lapel pins.

Brit Hume

If you don't like something, change it. If you can't change it, change your attitude.

Maya Angelou

If you have a positive attitude and constantly strive to give your best effort, eventually you will overcome your immediate problems and find you are ready for greater challenges.

Pat Riley

Style is a reflection of your attitude and your personality.

Shawn Ashmore

I believe if you keep your faith, you keep your trust, you keep the right attitude, if you're grateful, you'll see God open up new doors.

Joel Osteen

Your attitude is like a box of crayons that color your world. Constantly color your picture gray, and your picture will always be bleak. Try adding some bright colors to the picture by including humor, and your picture begins to lighten up.

Allen Klein

If you don't like something, change it. If you can't change it, change your attitude. Don't complain.

Maya Angelou

I believe that a trusting attitude and a patient attitude go hand in hand. You see, when you let go and learn to trust God, it releases joy in your life. And when you trust God, you're able to be more patient. Patience is not just about waiting for something... it's about how you wait, or your attitude while waiting.

Joyce Meyer

Success or failure depends more upon attitude than upon capacity successful men act as though they have accomplished or are enjoying something. Soon it becomes a reality. Act, look, feel successful, conduct yourself accordingly, and you will be amazed at the positive results.

William James

It is very important to generate a good attitude, a good heart, as much as possible. From this, happiness in both the short term and the long term for both yourself and others will come.

Dalai Lama

Sales are contingent upon the attitude of the salesman - not the attitude of the prospect.

W. Clement Stone

America needs to understand Islam, because this is the one religion that erases from its society the race problem. Throughout my travels in the Muslim world, I have met, talked to, even eaten with people who in America would have been considered 'white,' but the 'white' attitude had been removed from their minds by the religion of Islam.

Malcolm X

There's nothing better than having a baby. I've always loved children. I used to work summers at the YMCA and be in charge of, like, 30 preschool kids. I knew that when I had a child, I'd be overwhelmed, and it's true... I can't tell you how much my attitude has changed since we've got Frances. Holding my baby is the best drug in the world.

Kurt Cobain

The only disability in life is a bad attitude.

Scott Hamilton

A healthy attitude is contagious but don't wait to catch it from others. Be a carrier.

Tom Stoppard

There is little difference in people, but that little difference makes a big difference. That little difference is attitude. The big difference is whether it is positive or negative.

W. Clement Stone

The greatest discovery of all time is that a person can change his future by merely changing his attitude.

Oprah Winfrey

Watch out for the joy-stealers: gossip, criticism, complaining, faultfinding, and a negative, judgmental attitude.

Joyce Meyer

The higher the better. It's more about an attitude. High heels empower women in a way.

Christian Louboutin

Too much self-centered attitude, you see, brings, you see, isolation. Result: loneliness, fear, anger. The extreme self-centered attitude is the source of suffering.

Dalai Lama

Be sure what you want and be sure about yourself. Fashion is not just beauty, it's about good attitude. You have to believe in yourself and be strong.

Adriana Lima

I will keep smiling, be positive and never give up! I will give 100 percent each time I play. These are always my goals and my attitude.

Yani Tseng

When I was a child I asked my mother what homosexuality was about and she said - and this was 100 years ago in Germany and she was very open-minded - 'It's like hair color. It's nothing. Some people are blond and some people have dark hair. It's not a subject.' This was a very healthy attitude.

Karl Lagerfeld

It's easy to get negative because you get beat down. You go through a few disappointments and it's easy to stay in that negative frame of mind. Choosing to be positive and having a grateful attitude is a whole cliche, but your attitude is going to determine how you're going to live your life.

Joel Osteen

The best way to inspire people to superior performance is to convince them by everything you do and by your everyday attitude that you are wholeheartedly supporting them.

Harold S. Geneen

Today's students can put dope in their veins or hope in their brains. If they can conceive it and believe it, they can achieve it. They must know it is not their aptitude but their attitude that will determine their altitude.

Jesse Jackson

A positive attitude is something everyone can work on, and everyone can learn how to employ it.

Joan Lunden

Virtually nothing is impossible in this world if you just put your mind to it and maintain a positive attitude.

Lou Holtz

Happiness doesn't depend on any external conditions, it is governed by our mental attitude.

Dale Carnegie

Fairness is not an attitude. It's a professional skill that must be developed and exercised.

Brit Hume

Attitude is more important than the past, than education, than money, than circumstances, than what people do or say. It is more important than appearance, giftedness, or skill.

Charles R. Swindoll

Leadership is practiced not so much in words as in attitude and in actions.

Harold S. Geneen

I think people feel threatened by homosexuality. The problem isn't about gay people, the problem is about the attitude towards gay people. People think that all gays are Hannibal

Lecters. But gay people are sons and daughters, politicians and doctors, American heroes and daughters of American heroes.

Hollis Stacy

There's always the motivation of wanting to win. Everybody has that. But a champion needs, in his attitude, a motivation above and beyond winning.

Pat Riley

Like success, failure is many things to many people. With Positive Mental Attitude, failure is a learning experience, a rung on the ladder, a plateau at which to get your thoughts in order and prepare to try again.

W. Clement Stone

A lot of times I find that people who are blessed with the most talent don't ever develop that attitude, and the ones who aren't blessed in that way are the most competitive and have the biggest heart.

Tom Brady

Happiness is in our own hearts. I have no regrets of anything in the past. I'm totally cheerful and happy, and I think that a lot of your attitude is not in the circumstances you find yourself in, but in the circumstances you make for yourself.

Maeve Binchy

Woman must have her freedom, the fundamental freedom of choosing whether or not she will be a mother and how many children she will have. Regardless of what man's attitude may be, that problem is hers - and before it can be his, it is hers alone.

Margaret Sanger

A fit body gives you confidence. And there's nothing more impressive than a great attitude, which you can wear on your sleeve. But you'll have to remember the difference between being rude and being confident.

Virat Kohli

Everything I do, writing, touring, travelling, it all comes from the punk and hardcore attitude, from that expression - from being open to try things but relying on yourself, taking what you have into the battle and making of it what you will, hoping you can figure it out as you go. Make some sense of it.

Henry Rollins

Spend some time this weekend on home improvement; improve your attitude toward your family.

Bo Bennett

Chaotic people often have chaotic lives, and I think they create that. But if you try and have an inner peace and a positive attitude, I think you attract that.

Imelda Staunton

The winner's edge is not in a gifted birth, a high IQ, or in talent. The winner's edge is all in the attitude, not aptitude. Attitude is the criterion for success.

Denis Waitley

Mental attitude and concentration are the keys to pitching.

Ferguson Jenkins

Always go into meetings or negotiations with a positive attitude. Tell yourself you're going to make this the best deal for all parties.

Natalie Massenet

Excellence is not a skill, it's an attitude.

Ralph Marston

When you have vision it affects your attitude. Your attitude is optimistic rather than pessimistic.

Charles R. Swindoll

I enjoy punk, the attitude as well as the music, but I don't feel like I have to be a carbon copy of it and invite all this controversy just to be punk rock.

Hayley Williams

It's sort of a mental attitude about critical thinking and curiosity. It's about mindset of looking at the world in a playful and curious and creative way.

Adam Savage

Being black is not a matter of pigmentation - being black is a reflection of a mental attitude.

Steven Biko

No rational argument will have a rational effect on a man who does not want to adopt a rational attitude.

Karl Popper

A strong positive mental attitude will create more miracles than any wonder drug.

Patricia Neal

Hope is favorable and confident expectation; it's an expectant attitude that something good is going to happen and things will work out, no matter what situation we're facing.

Joyce Meyer

Having a clear faith, based on the creed of the church is often labeled today as fundamentalism. Whereas relativism, which is letting oneself be tossed and swept along by every wind of teaching, look like the only attitude acceptable to today's standards.

Pope Benedict XVI

Vanity, showing off, is an attitude that reduces spirituality to a worldly thing, which is the worst sin that could be committed in the church.

Pope Francis

My attitude to peace is rather based on the Burmese definition of peace - it really means removing all the negative factors that destroy peace in this world. So peace does not mean just putting an end to violence or to war, but to all other factors that threaten peace, such as discrimination, such as inequality, poverty.

Aung San Suu Kyi

Any fact facing us is not as important as our attitude toward it, for that determines our success or failure. The way you think about a fact may defeat you before you ever do anything about it. You are overcome by the fact because you think you are.

Norman Vincent Peale

You can't study comedy; it's within you. It's a personality. My humor is an attitude.

Don Rickles

I think a lot of times we don't pay enough attention to people with a positive attitude because we assume they are naive or stupid or unschooled.

Amy Adams

I wouldn't ever say if you're having tough times then there must be something wrong with you or your attitude. Life's a fight. It's a good fight of faith. I encourage people to stay up, stay hopeful, stay faith-filled.

Joel Osteen

You get tough when you grow up unloved. People described me as a boyish girl - rather shy, but I didn't show it. I had an attitude. I was rather wild. I lied a lot because I knew the alternative was to be punished. As I got older I realised I didn't have to lie any more and it was a nice feeling. I could be myself.

Maj Sjowall

The prevailing - and foolish - attitude is that a good manager can be a good manager anywhere, with no special knowledge of the production process he's managing. A man with a financial background may know nothing about manufacturing shoes or cars, but he's put in charge anyway.

W. Edwards Deming

So long as you've got your friends about you, and a good positive attitude, you don't really have to care what everyone else thinks.

Gail Porter

I think music is the greatest art form that exists, and I think people listen to music for different reasons, and it serves different purposes. Some of it is background music, and some of it is things that might affect a person's day, if not their life, or change an attitude. The best songs are the ones that make you feel something.

Eddie Vedder

My attitude is never to be satisfied, never enough, never.

Duke Ellington

By making a comeback, I'm changing the attitude of people toward me. If I'd known that people would react so enthusiastically, I'd have done it years ago.

Mark Spitz

Regardless of what one's attitude towards prohibition may be, temperance is something against which, at a time of war, no reasonable protest can be made.

William Lyon Mackenzie King

Being deeply contented with God in my everyday life is a focused attitude. It is always available. It means practicing letting go of my obsession with how I'm doing. It means training myself to learn to actually be present with people, and seeking to love them.

John Ortberg

Attitude is attitude, whether you're a West Coast gangster or East Coast gangster, you know?

Paul Walker

I've reached a point in my life where it's the little things that matter... I was always a rebel and probably could have got much farther had I changed my attitude. But when you think about it, I got pretty far without changing attitudes. I'm happier with that.

Veronica Lake

Tackle the difficult things first in the morning; make changes in the way you network. Treat everyone with respect and dignity. This stops you from cynicism and negativity. End your day with that same attitude you started. Renew your contract with a day well completed.

Rick Pitino

I have a very positive attitude in life. My insecurity, fear and need to know about tomorrow has fortunately eased. What is going to happen will happen anyway. So why break my head over it?

Katrina Kaif

No matter what the recipe, any baker can do wonders in the kitchen with some good ingredients and an upbeat attitude!

Buddy Valastro

I have a very positive attitude to anyone who is protecting the environment, but it's inadmissible when people are using it as a means of promoting themselves, using it as a source of self-enrichment. I don't want to name any specific examples... but often, environmentalism is used to blackmail companies.

Vladimir Putin

Could we change our attitude, we should not only see life differently, but life itself would come to be different.

Katherine Mansfield

There is no attitude required. The hat brings the attitude. And when people try on a hat they like, it is a bit of fun. It makes them laugh. You don't laugh when you put on a pair of shoes, but you do with a hat.

Philip Treacy

Hitler and Mussolini were only the primary spokesmen for the attitude of domination and craving for power that are in the heart of almost everyone. Until the source is cleared, there will always be confusion and hate, wars and class antagonisms.

Jiddu Krishnamurti

You know, I always say white is not a colour, white is an attitude, and if you haven't got trillions of dollars in the bank that you don't need, you can't be white.

Dick Gregory

You can do everything you can to try to stop bad things from happening to you, but eventually things will happen, so the best prevention is a positive attitude.

Marie Osmond

Always keep that happy attitude. Pretend that you are holding a beautiful fragrant bouquet.

Earl Nightingale

A great attitude does much more than turn on the lights in our worlds; it seems to magically connect us to all sorts of serendipitous opportunities that were somehow absent before the change.

Earl Nightingale

Success or failure in business is caused more by the mental attitude even than by mental capacities.

Walter Scott

Being a sex symbol has to do with an attitude, not looks. Most men think it's looks, most women know otherwise.

Kathleen Turner

I don't think punk ever really dies, because punk rock attitude can never die.

Billy Idol

Vampires are so old that they don't need to impress anyone anymore. They're comfortable in their own skin. It's this enigmatic strength that's very romantic and old-fashioned. I think it goes back to something of a Victorian attitude of finding a strong man who's going to look after his woman.

Stephen Moyer

Black Consciousness is an attitude of the mind and a way of life, the most positive call to emanate from the black world for a long time.

Steven Biko

There is a need for financial reform along ethical lines that would produce in its turn an economic reform to benefit everyone. This would nevertheless require a courageous change of attitude on the part of political leaders.

Pope Francis

All we need, really, is a change from a near frigid to a tropical attitude of mind.

Marjory Stoneman Douglas

I think the best advice came from Drew Barrymore, about always finding love in everything you do and keeping a positive attitude and being thankful.

Bella Thorne

Crime is terribly revealing. Try and vary your methods as you will, your tastes, your habits, your attitude of mind, and your soul is revealed by your actions.

Agatha Christie

An attitude to life which seeks fulfillment in the single-minded pursuit of wealth - in short, materialism - does not fit into this world, because it contains within itself no limiting principle, while the environment in which it is placed is strictly limited.

E. F. Schumacher

Culture is very important to the Mavs. Your best player has to be a fit for what you want the culture of the team to be. He has to be someone who leads by example. Someone who sets the tone in the locker room and on the court. It isn't about who talks the most or the loudest. It is about the demeanor and attitude he brings.

Mark Cuban

Some people say that I have an attitude- Maybe I do. But I think that you have to. You have to believe in yourself when no one else does- that makes you a winner right there.

Venus Williams

Every small business will give you an entrepreneurial way of looking at things. I guarantee you that for every plant that closes, if you gave it to one small-business person in that community, he or she would find a way to make it work. The small-business attitude is you always find a way to make it work.

Hamdi Ulukaya

We can revolutionize the attitude of inner city brown and black kids to learning. We need a civil rights movement within the African-American community.

Henry Louis Gates

I think it's important and I think it's true that our life experience is going to be about our attitude, our thoughts, our beliefs, our speech and our actions. We can transform our life experience simply by changing our language.

Jason Mraz

Hence, within the space of two generations there has been a complete revolution in the attitude of the trades-unions toward the women working in their trades.

Florence Kelley

If you have fun and keep a good attitude, people want to work with you.

James Marsden

If you want small changes in your life, work on your attitude. But if you want big and primary changes, work on your paradigm.

Stephen Covey

Negative attitude is nine times more powerful than positive attitude.

Bikram Choudhury

I was looking for something a lot heavier, yet melodic at the same time. Something different from heavy metal, a different attitude.

Kurt Cobain

And the attitude of faith is the very opposite of clinging to belief, of holding on.

Alan Watts

I have played on many teams throughout my career, and I know when a team has the tools, and the right positive attitude towards winning.

Boomer Esiason

Commitment, belief and positive attitude are all important if you're going to be a success, whether you're in sports, in business or, as in my case, anthropology.

Donald Johanson

Everybody is a political person, whether you say something or you are silent. A political attitude is not whether you go to parliament; it's how you deal with your life, with your surroundings.

Paulo Coelho

You may not be able to change a situation, but with humor you can change your attitude about it.

Allen Klein

If somebody says no to you, or if you get cut, Michael Jordan was cut his first year, but he came back and he was the best ever. That is what you have to have. The attitude that I'm going to show everybody, I'm going to work hard to get better and better.

Magic Johnson

The ABC's are attitude, behavior and communication skills.

Gerald Chertavian

Animals have a much better attitude to life and death than we do. They know when their time has come. We are the ones that suffer when they pass, but it's a healing kind of grief that enables us to deal with other griefs that are not so easy to grab hold of.

Emmylou Harris

I do have moments when I feel insecure. I do have moments when I feel jealous, and that's normal. It's a very normal emotion. It's your action and your attitude and your reaction to that that is important.

Anushka Sharma

It's great to be somewhat of a role model. I want to be a positive and good role model and lead by example and try to do the best I can. Playing good golf definitely draws attention, but I want to have a good attitude on the course and do the right things.

Rickie Fowler

One's appearance bespeaks dignity corresponding to the depth of his character. One's concentrated effort, serene attitude, taciturn air, courteous disposition, thoroughly polite bearing, gritted teeth with a piercing look - each of these reveals dignity. Such outward appearance, in short, comes from constant attentiveness and seriousness.

Yamamoto Tsunetomo

I always said punk was an attitude. It was never about having a Mohican haircut or wearing a ripped T-shirt. It was all about destruction, and the creative potential within that.

Malcolm Mclaren

Some of us pray demands. Some of us pray complaints. Some of us pray knowing, and some of us pray not knowing. But prayer is the attitude that you hold in your heart.

Iyanla Vanzant

Meekness implies a spirit of gratitude as opposed to an attitude of self-sufficiency, an acknowledgement of a greater power beyond oneself, a recognition of God, and an acceptance of his commandments.

Gordon B. Hinckley

My mom had me at 16 and took me every place she went. I remember going on peace marches. She tried to take me to Woodstock - it was pouring rain. It was on my birthday, and I was crying so much in the car they turned the car around and dumped me at my grandmother's house... I had a little attitude.

Debi Mazar

I think clothes are very much a representation of your attitude and the way you feel. I really love to be dressed down, though.

Trey Songz

There was always a feeling for me that it would work. That's what keeps me going. You go in with a positive attitude and stay there, and that's a big part of what does make it work.

Shelley Long

I was born with an extremely negative attitude. I was the kid who wouldn't smile in Christmas photos, was a poor sport, and hated a lot of things. I eventually grew out of my negativity when I matured.

Colton Haynes

A smart manager will establish a culture of gratitude. Expand the appreciative attitude to suppliers, vendors, delivery people, and of course, customers.

Harvey Mackay

There is a brief moment when all there is in a man's mind and soul and spirit is reflected through his eyes, his hands, his attitude. This is the moment to record.

Yousuf Karsh

Certain thoughts are prayers. There are moments when, whatever be the attitude of the body, the soul is on its knees.

Victor Hugo

Solidarity is an attitude of resistance, I suppose, or it should be.

Christopher Hitchens

Every child's taste is different. Don't worry if they're not reading 'War and Peace' at age 12. First, build a good foundation and a positive attitude about reading by letting them pick the stories they enjoy. Make friends with a bookseller or librarian. They are a wealth of information on finding books that kids enjoy.

Rick Riordan

Whatever your situation might be, set your mind to whatever you want to do and put a good attitude in it, and I believe that you can succeed. You are not going to get anywhere just sitting on your butt and moping around.

Bethany Hamilton

You tell your kids that no matter what, you set your goals and you go for them. Whatever it is you achieve, never give up. You want your kids to have that good attitude, the confidence, and the will power to believe in themselves.

Joel Parkinson

Your attitude towards failure determines your altitude after failure.

John C. Maxwell

You call to a dog and a dog will break its neck to get to you. Dogs just want to please. Call to a cat and its attitude is, 'What's in it for me?'

Lewis Grizzard

Prayer is talking with God. God knows your heart and is not so concerned with your words as He is with the attitude of your heart.

Josh McDowell

Design is about point of view, and there should be some sort of woman or lifestyle or attitude in one's head as a designer.

Vera Wang

Players should know that if you can't make the contribution of the winning shot, that your attitude every day when you come to practice, or the positive contribution you make through cheering and keeping up team morale, is just as important in the overall picture.

Sue Wicks

It goes without saying that the Jewish people can have no other goal than Palestine and that, whatever the fate of the proposition may be, our attitude toward the land of our fathers is and shall remain unchangeable.

Theodor Herzl

I have always detested any departure from reality, an attitude which I relate to my mother's poor mental health.

Jean Piaget

All punk is is attitude. That's what makes it. The attitude.

Joey Ramone

My attitude is always one of sensuality, aggressive enthusiasm and a kind of outrageousness in my expression.

Sally Kirkland

There is definitely something sexy about a girl with an attitude and a pair of leather pants.

Eliza Dushku

Being made to feel like an irrelevant child was probably an asset. Benign negligence is not a bad parental attitude or at least a cross between a benevolent dictator and benign negligence - you should just let kids crack on with it.

Clare Balding

When you're walking at the airport, you're expected to smile at people because they know you... I find that tough. I'm only trying to protect myself. So I don't take my eyes off the floor. People can take that as attitude. But it's actually shyness. Yes, it is a bad habit. But it's a defense mechanism.

Katrina Kaif

You need an attitude of service. You're not just serving yourself. You help others to grow up and you grow with them.

David Green

Any of us can be happy and have a good attitude when everything is going our way. But I believe it's the real test of your character and of your faith to say, 'Things are not going our way, but I'm still being good to people; I'm still attending church; I still have a good attitude.'

Joel Osteen

Choosing an attitude of faith will release peace out of your spirit and into your soul.

Joyce Meyer

If someone you know makes a bad decision or uses bad judgment, it doesn't mean you have to allow that to alter your attitude. Why should you allow anyone else's bad decisions to send you into a tailspin of misery?

Joyce Meyer

When a person doesn't have gratitude, something is missing in his or her humanity. A person can almost be defined by his or her attitude toward gratitude.

Elie Wiesel

I am responsible. Although I may not be able to prevent the worst from happening, I am responsible for my attitude toward the inevitable misfortunes that darken life.

Walter Anderson

I have so many indie bands on my iPod. What I don't really understand is the attitude that if a band is unknown, they're good, and if they get fans, then you move on to the next band.

Taylor Swift

At home in Ireland, there's a habit of avoidance, an ironical attitude towards the authority figure.

Seamus Heaney

Not every religion has to have St. Augustine's attitude to sex. Why even in our culture marriages are celebrated in a church, everyone present knows what is going to happen that night, but that doesn't prevent it being a religious ceremony.

Ludwig Wittgenstein

Liberalism is an attitude rather than a set of dogmas - an attitude that insists upon questioning all plausible and self-evident propositions, seeking not to reject them but to find out what evidence there is to support them rather than their possible alternatives.

Morris Raphael Cohen

To make flexibility work, it is not only necessary to change our attitude about who is a good worker and who is not, but we have to train managers at all levels to recognize the difference between the number of hours worked and the quality of work produced.

Madeleine M. Kunin

In the business world today, failure is apparently not an option. We need to change this attitude toward failure - and celebrate the idea that only by falling on our collective business faces do we learn enough to succeed down the road.

Naveen Jain

The attitude that nature is chaotic and that the artist puts order into it is a very absurd point of view, I think. All that we can hope for is to put some order into ourselves.

Willem de Kooning

Never refuse an assignment except when there is a conflict of interest, a potential of danger to you or your family, or you hold a strongly biased attitude about the subject under focus.

Jessica Savitch

All the champions - you go and ask Mike Tyson or Joe Louis, Rocky Marciano, Lennox Lewis and myself included, and I'm sorry for putting myself in line with all the other great names - but the champion's attitude is it doesn't matter who is in front of me, I am going to conquer this person and win the fight and knock the person out.

Wladimir Klitschko

What sculptors do is represent the essence of gesture. What is important in mime is attitude.

Marcel Marceau

The time I spent thinking about how I was better than somebody else or worrying about somebody else's attitude was time I could put to better use.

Charley Pride

I'm not a model; hence I don't see the reason to have a six-pack abs. I can pull off a tough and rugged look of a cop in 'Dhoom' series without taking my shirt off. Cops don't have to move around without a shirt to flaunt their machismo. What makes the character of a cop stand out is his attitude and not his six-pack abs.

Abhishek Bachchan

I have an attitude. It's what I do. I'm edgy. I have an attitude.

Hope Solo

A lot can be said with just a look, or the way the body moves. Each song is a different character. So each song takes on a different movement of the body. And the body has to go with the subject and the attitude that you have toward that subject.

Eartha Kitt

I love festivals because they seem like more of an artsy, supportive attitude - which benefits a more theatrical performer sometimes with having theater and other non-club venues, as well as the audience being filled with other artists. It's nice to be with other comics, as usually at other road gigs, I'm solo for the most part.

Maria Bamford

Modern Orthodoxy has a highly positive attitude toward the State of Israel. Our Ultra-Orthodox brethren recognize only the Holy Land, but not the state.

Norman Lamm

The pool is terrible, but that doesn't have much to do with my record swims. That's all mental attitude.

Mark Spitz

It's not just a matter of poor willpower on the part of the consumer and a give-the-people-what-they-want attitude on the part of the food manufacturers. What I found, over four years of research and reporting, was a conscious effort... to get people hooked on foods that are convenient and inexpensive.

Michael Moss

I started modeling when I was - not older, but not 12. I have a mom who's a feminist - she's an English professor, an intellectual. She really gave me the equipment to understand that you can celebrate yourself without putting yourself down or needing to apologize for the way you look. I think that attitude is really crucial for a model.

Emily Ratajkowski

We awaken in others the same attitude of mind we hold toward them.

Elbert Hubbard

It will be disastrous when a leader or manager shows up with one attitude one day and treats people with a different attitude the next day.

Zig Ziglar

People in tough times - it doesn't mean they don't have a great attitude.

Joel Osteen

I believe that when you think of the negative, and you get up discouraged - 'There's nothing good in my future' - I really believe it almost ties the hands of God. God works where there's an attitude of faith. I believe faith is all about hope.

Joel Osteen

If a person gets his attitude toward money straight, it will help straighten out almost every other area in his life.

Billy Graham

Reproach is shame, blame, disgrace, disapproval and a disrespectful attitude toward yourself. When you're under reproach, your behavior shows it.

Joyce Meyer

There must be something solemn, serious, and tender about any attitude which we denominate religious. If glad, it must not grin or snicker; if sad, it must not scream or curse.

William James

I want to look my best for God. So many people have the attitude that if you're a Christian you've got to dress bad, wear an old color, not do anything to your hair, have nothing. It's no wonder that Christianity is not very attractive. I mean, how many people do you know in a Western culture that's going to go, 'Yeah, give me some of that?'

Joyce Meyer

We submit to the majority because we have to. But we are not compelled to call our attitude of subjection a posture of respect.

Ambrose Bierce

I am Classic Rock Revisited. I revisit it every waking moment of my life because it has the spirit and the attitude and the fire and the middle finger. I am Rosa Parks with a Gibson guitar.

Ted Nugent

Our judgments judge us, and nothing reveals us, exposes our weaknesses, more ingeniously than the attitude of pronouncing upon our fellows.

Paul Valery

I was born with a happy heart, and I try to keep a good attitude. It's not true that I'm happy all the time because nobody is, and we all go through our things.

Dolly Parton

Mankind's true moral test, its fundamental test (which lies deeply buried from view), consists of its attitude towards those who are at its mercy: animals. And in this respect mankind has suffered a fundamental debacle, a debacle so fundamental that all others stem from it.

Milan Kundera

The purely agitational attitude is not good enough for a detailed consideration of a subject.

Jawaharlal Nehru

Whenever I'm having a bad day and have an attitude, I stay home. I keep it at home.

Michael Clarke Duncan

It is precisely the purpose of the public opinion generated by the press to make the public incapable of judging, to insinuate into it the attitude of someone irresponsible, uninformed.

Walter Benjamin

We live in a country that used to have a can-do attitude, and now we have a 'what-can-you-do-for-me?' attitude, and what I try to do is find ways that we can develop common ground.

Benjamin Carson

Stiletto, I look at it more as an attitude as opposed to a high-heeled shoe.

Lita Ford

There is a soak-the-rich attitude in the air, a feeling that if you have a lot of money you must have got it by some ghastly means. I can quite happily say there was never any family money. All the money we got was mine, just from writing books.

Terry Pratchett

I love everybody. One of the great things about me is that I have a very positive attitude.

Imelda Marcos

My grandfather was a man, when he talked about freedom, his attitude was really interesting. His view was that you had obligations or you had responsibilities, and when you fulfilled those obligations or responsibilities, that then gave you the liberty to do other things.

Clarence Thomas

If you want my personal attitude, I would tell you that I don't care about a person's sexual orientation.

Vladimir Putin

I was kicked out of school because of my attitude. I was not assimilating. So I went to work, taking any jobs I could get.

Richard Pryor

You can't start a movie by having the attitude that the script is finished, because if you think the script is finished, your movie is finished before the first day of shooting.

Steven Spielberg

What is worthy or unworthy on the Sabbath day will have to be judged by each of us by trying to be honest with the Lord. On the Sabbath day, we should do what we have to do and what we ought to do in an attitude of worshipfulness and then limit our other activities.

James E. Faust

I separated from the Southern Baptists when they adopted the discriminatory attitude towards women, because I believe what Paul taught in Galatians that there is no distinction in God's eyes between men and women, slaves and masters, Jews and non-Jews - everybody is created equally in the eyes of God.

Jimmy Carter

I don't think it's a good attitude in your life to feel that you have to be rich to have self-esteem.

Tom Petty

I think it's your mental attitude. So many of us start dreading age in high school and that's a waste of a lovely life. 'Oh... I'm 30, oh, I'm 40, oh, 50.' Make the most of it.

Betty White

I keep guitars that are, you know, the neck's a little bit bent and it's a little bit out of tune. I want to work and battle it and conquer it and make it express whatever attitude I have at that moment. I want it to be a struggle.

Jack White

What matters to me is that I do what I think is right and I see, I'm a numbers guy, that's my attitude. I know we have a debt tsunami coming, we are bankrupting this country and I'm in a position where I can actually advance ideas to prevent that from happening. That's exactly what I should be doing.

Paul Ryan

Pessimism only describes an attitude, and not facts, and hence is entirely subjective.

Francis Parker Yockey

All women have appealing features. I do not refer to model-type appeal, but rather that which comes from your personality, your attitude, and your expressions. I urge you to enhance the natural, God-given, feminine gifts with which you have been so richly blessed.

James E. Faust

Today's youth are told to get rich or die trying and they really shouldn't take that attitude forward with them.

Kareem Abdul-Jabbar

I mean, the shoe - there is a music to it, there is attitude, there is sound, it's a movement. Clothes - it's a different story. There are a million things I'd rather do before designing clothes: directing, landscaping.

Christian Louboutin

I was impressed by Hendrix. His attitude was brilliant. Even the way he walked was amazing.

Ritchie Blackmore

I have this theory that, depending on your attitude, your life doesn't have to become this ridiculous charade that it seems so many people end up living.

Christian Bale

We assume that we've come so far as compassionate citizens of the world if we do choose to read the news, yet the attitude towards life can be one where we put blinders on and forget that there are civil wars going on. It's easy to forget that there are so many people starving to death every single day.

Anne Hathaway

Money brings you security and choice. You can make decisions in a different way if you have a lot of money. But when you have nothing, you have a naivety, and a more fearless attitude because you have nothing to lose.

Simon Cowell

Age and size are only numbers. It's the attitude you bring to clothes that make the difference.

Donna Karan

That's what I love from metal, and that's what I love from hip-hop. That's what I love from any music that's hard, that's got an edge to it-The attitude in it.

Kid Rock

Being a part of SKECHERS is exciting. It is such a hip company with a great attitude and image.

Carrie Underwood

I think failure is nothing more than life's way of nudging you that you are off course. My attitude to failure is not attached to outcome, but in not trying. It is liberating. Most people attach failure to something not working out or how people perceive you. This way, it is about answering to yourself.

Sara Blakely

And I tell you, having girls has made me a much better man. I have friends who are fathers, but they only have boys, and they have the same attitude toward women they always had, you know? And I don't play that... My girls, you mess with them? I will bury you underground.

Mark Wahlberg

My father was an engineer and my mother was a social worker, and they met as young socialists. That probably tells you everything you need to know about my attitude to money - I've never really been bothered about it.

Jo Brand

The novelist teaches the reader to comprehend the world as a question. There is wisdom and tolerance in that attitude. In a world built on sacrosanct certainties the novel is dead.

Milan Kundera

Yes, we're still five little people with a noisy attitude.

Angus Young

The Dolls were an attitude. If nothing else they were a great attitude.

Johnny Thunders

What is required as we travel towards full unemployment is not new legislation but a gradual change of mental attitude, a shift in values. As our taste for idling grows, we will refuse to work for old-fashioned bosses who demand a five-day, 40-hour, nine-to-five type week, or worse.

Tom Hodgkinson

Most of my arguments with musicians through the years have had more to do with their attitude about music, or their attitude about their own lives, or their personal responsibility. Music has never really been the big centerpiece of the fight.

Billy Corgan

It's a fundamental, social attitude that the 1% supports symphonies and operas and doesn't support Johnny learning to program hip-hop beats. When I put it like that, it sounds like, 'Well, yeah,' but you start to think, 'Why not, though?' What makes one more valuable than another?

David Byrne

If you can't change your fate, change your attitude.

Charles Revson

If you have an ongoing relationship with a person, think of everything positive about that person that you possibly can and enter your interaction from that space. Ignore all the crap that used to drive you up the wall before. You will be amazed at what a change this attitude shift brings about.

Srikumar Rao

The purely agitation attitude is not good enough for a detailed consideration of a subject.

Michael Korda

As a child, I was aware of the widely-held attitude that the ocean is so big, so resilient that we could use the sea as the ultimate place to dispose of anything we did not want, from garbage and nuclear wastes to sludge from sewage to entire ships that had reached the end of their useful life.

Sylvia Earle

Italian style is a natural attitude. It is about a life of good taste. It doesn't have to be expensive. Simple but with good taste. Luxury is possible to buy. Good taste is not.

Diego Della Valle

My denial and irresponsible attitude about asthma put me at great risk and caused me so much needless suffering. My hope is that the kids I talk to learn to open up about their asthma, become educated about their condition, and seek help.

Jackie Joyner-Kersee

When a parent shows up with an attitude of entitlement, understand that under it is a boatload of anxiety.

Robert Evans

The attitude of insolent haughtiness is characteristic of the relationships Americans form with what is alien to them, with others.

Jose Saramago

I was fortunate to play for Pete Rose and have teammates like Ken Griffey Sr., Tony Perez and Dave Concepcion. I grew up in the game with a mature attitude. I've always known it was better to be seen and not heard.

Eric Davis

I look at Jagger and the like and if I see a good attitude I'll admire it but I wouldn't copy their style.

Michael Hutchence

That attitude that fighting is probably not fair, but you have to defend yourself anyway and damage the enemy, has been profoundly consequential as far as my political activism goes.

June Jordan

You don't have to have an attitude if you're famous.

Adriana Lima

My second husband believed I had such a fickle attitude to friendship that each Friday he would update the list of my 'Top Ten' friends in the manner of a Top Of The Pops chart countdown.

Julie Burchill

Gardening is not trivial. If you believe that it is, closely examine why you feel that way. You may discover that this attitude has been forced upon you by mass media and the crass culture it creates and maintains. The fact is, gardening is just the opposite - it is, or should be, a central, basic expression of human life.

Andrew Weil

Attitude is your acceptance of the natural laws, or your rejection of the natural laws.

Stuart Chase

It was my father who instilled the 'never say no' attitude I carry around with me today, and who instilled in me a sense of wonder, always taking us on adventures in the car, never telling us the destination.

Marlee Matlin

I'm not a person who writes really abstract things with oblique references. I look at abstraction like I look at condiments. Give me some Tabasco sauce, some ketchup, some mayonnaise. I love all of that. Put it on a trumpet. I've just got to have the ketchup and Tabasco sauce. That's my attitude about musical philosophy.

Wynton Marsalis

Quite honestly, if we do manage to destroy the planet with our devil-may-care attitude to natural resources, I'd suggest we leave, as a dossier in our defence, the collected letters to agony aunts and uncles down the generations. It would certainly prove that we weren't all bad!

Mariella Frostrup

What was past was past. I suppose that was the general attitude.

V. S. Naipaul

An aristocratic culture does not advertise its emotions. In its forms of expression it is sober and reserved. Its general attitude is stoic.

Johan Huizinga

I tend to be pessimistic about everything: If things seem to be going good, I'm worried that it's going to end; if things are bad, then I'm worried that it's going to be permanent. It's not a very comfortable attitude to have all the time.

Jesse Eisenberg

From the very early stage when I started doing performance art in the '70s, the general attitude - not just me, but also my colleagues - was that there should not be any documentation, that the performance itself is artwork and there should be no documentation.

Marina Abramovic

I'm not going to take this defeatist attitude and listen to all this crap any more from all these people who have nothing except doomsday to predict.

Carroll Shelby

Seek out that particular mental attribute which makes you feel most deeply and vitally alive, along with which comes the inner voice which says, 'This is the real me,' and when you have found that attitude, follow it.

James Truslow Adams

There is a single thread of attitude, a single direction of flow, that joins our present time to its early burgeoning in Mediterranean civilization.

Arthur Erickson

My mother, she had a very good attitude toward money. I'm very grateful for the fact that we had to learn to save. I used to get like 50 pence a week, and I'd save it for like five months. And then I'd spend it on Christmas presents. I'd save up like eight pounds. It's nothing, but we did that.

Gemma Arterton

From the beginning, I've always had a knack for catchy melodies. But I went through a period when I was trying to be rock n' roll and have a rock n' roll attitude. I was fighting my nature by trying to play really hard and sing really hard. But at a certain point, I realized that I loved syrupy pop music with tons of harmony.

Juliana Hatfield

My attitude towards drawing is not necessarily about drawing. It's about making the best kind of image I can make, it's about talking as clearly as I can.

Jim Dine

My deepest impulses are optimistic, an attitude that seems to me as spiritually necessary and proper as it is intellectually suspect.

Ellen Willis

In individual industries where female labour pays an important role, any movement advocating better wages, shorter working hours, etc., would not be doomed from the start because of the attitude of those women workers who are not organized.

Clara Zetkin

It is possible for the assembly-line worker consigned to tightening the bolts on the transmission and the office worker who processes medical insurance claims to work with pride and efficiency, but it's not easy to maintain that attitude.

Paul Hawken

Like the Earth, the Web is a less appealing place than it used to be. If I want attitude and arguing and meanness and profanity and wrong information screamed at me as gospel, I'll get in a time machine and spend Christmas with my family in 1977.

J. R. Moehringer

That term's definitely got a negative aura to it, because people think a diva is somebody with an attitude who demands things all the time. Of course there is that type of diva, but my idea of a diva has always been a singer - whether male or female - who gets on that stage and captivates you with their presence and their voice.

Jordin Sparks

Although as a sailor I despised politics - for I loved my sailor's life and still love it today - conditions forced me to take up a definite attitude towards political problems.

Fritz Sauckel

Mainly what I learned from Buddy... was an attitude. He loved music, and he taught me that it shouldn't have any barriers to it.

Waylon Jennings

I fell in love with Erica Kane the summer before my freshman year of high school. Like all red-blooded teen American boys, I'd come home from water polo practice and eat a box of Entenmann's Pop'Ems donut holes in front of the TV while obsessively fawning over 'All My Children' and Erica, her clothes, and her narcissistic attitude.

Andy Cohen

I'm not anti-fashion, but I've always had a bit of a punk attitude. That's important, I think. I do my own thing.

Sade Adu

Regardless of the gender of the highest wage earner, the balance of power in the relationship will suffer if the higher earner uses control of the purse strings as a system of reward and punishment. It will also suffer if the lower earner takes a chippy, haughty attitude to spending money they haven't actually generated themselves.

Marian Keyes

Given the scale of issues like global warming and epidemic disease, we shouldn't underestimate the importance of a can-do attitude to science rather than a can't-afford-it attitude.

Martin Rees

The fictionally correct have all the answers, and that's what's wrong with them. They're artistic technocrats. There's no dilemma so knotty, no question so baffling, that it can't be smoothly neutralized by dialing up the right attitude adjustment. Poor old Hemingway. If only he'd known.

Walter Kirn

I was bringing my attitude as a regular person 'cause this is my attitude.

Glenn Danzig

I've never been out with any of the cast of Coronation Street. We're all very close friends so it's very much a professional attitude.

Richard Fleeshman

People are patronizing the theatres with renewed enthusiasm - there is an entire picnic-like attitude when families go out to see movies, which is a very good sign. They want to see larger-than-life characters on the big screen and not just watch movies on television or on DVDs.

Salman Khan

I've always considered myself to be fiercely patriotic. I love Britain - its history and the down-to-earth attitude people have.

Gary Numan

Even if people do wrong, we're social animals, so what can we do about stopping them doing the same things in future? Saying people are 'bad' or 'evil' is just an unwillingness to engage; an unwillingness to try to empathise. That sanctimonious attitude doesn't help anyone.

Denise Mina

I think fun is an important part of the entertainment industry, and it should be. Anybody who's not incorporating some of that into their work needs to take a break, go away, and have an attitude adjustment.

Diane Lane

What irritates me is the bland way people go around saying, 'Oh, our attitude has changed. We don't dislike these people any more.' But by the strangest coincidence, they haven't taken away the injustice; the laws are still on the books.

Christopher Isherwood

All ideas come about through some sort of observation. It sparks an attitude; some object or emotion causes a reaction in the other person.

Graham Chapman

The pilot looked at his cues of attitude and speed and orientation and so on and responded as he would from the same cues in an airplane, but there was no way it flew the same. The simulators had showed us that.

Alan Shepard

As no one knew much about my mental illness, a lot of people had the attitude that I had the capability to 'kick it' and get better instantly. This was the most frustrating attitude for me.

Andy Behrman

I think one of the things that language poets are very involved with is getting away from conventional ideas of beauty, because those ideas contain a certain attitude toward women, certain attitudes toward sex, certain attitudes toward race, etc.

Diane Wakoski

There are so many myths out there about Marianne Faithfull, I had to, um, detach. But I can turn it on because Marianne Faithfull is really an attitude, you know.

Marianne Faithfull

I think that generally music should be a positive thing, I like Bob Marley's attitude: he said that his goal in life was to single handedly fight all the evil in the world with nothing but music, and when he went to a place he didn't go to play, he went to conquer.

Jon Fishman

We have the ability to craft a life where we are completely fulfilled. We think it is dependent on outsiders, and to some extent it is, but it is much more dependent on the attitude we bring to life.

Srikumar Rao

I grew up in a small, strictly-Catholic fishing village on the coast of Wales. The people there have a different attitude to life than those in Hollywood - people stick together more.

Catherine Zeta-Jones

I think I have a mental nappy attitude.

Paul Mooney

My agent says that I'm a 'repeat business guy.' If you hire me to come do a movie, I'll be on time, know all my material, be ready to go, have a good attitude. I'm here to work, so I get hired over and over again by the same producers. If you just be a team player on set you can work so much more often.

Dean Cain

Your attitude is contagious.

Kevin Plank

In Gnosticism, the physical world did not ultimately matter - which meant physical suffering did not matter either. Seeking 'enlightenment' meant cultivating an attitude of detachment, even indifference.

Nancy Pearcey

I want to work with kids and help develop them, show them the right way, the right morals and attitude into how to become a better footballer. Australia has many different cultures but I'd like to bring in the indigenous style, bring their competitiveness, athleticism and raw ability into the frame.

Timothy F. Cahill

In terms of work I've always had a Bad Attitude in that I won't work anywhere which requires me to work strict hours or follow a dress code. I don't know if that's an Asperger's thing or not, I think it's just being reasonable.

Bram Cohen

I have a political attitude, but I'm certainly not a politician.

Kgalema Motlanthe

Only one thing can conquer war - that attitude of mind which can see nothing in war but destruction and annihilation.

Ludwig von Mises

Life is about challenges and how we face up to them and the attitude we take into every day life so hopefully we'll be able to motivate people to do more with their life.

Martina Navratilova

We can do better in higher education. And it is more than just technology. It's also an attitude on the part of faculty. We need to think through how we can produce a better quality product at less cost.

Roy Romer

If a person can be said to have the wrong attitude, there is no need to pay attention to his arguments.

John McCarthy

I'd love to look like my mum when I am her age. She taught ballet for years, and my attitude to exercise and fitness has definitely been influenced by her. She's 84 now, and I've watched how well she has aged, and a lot of that is to do with her fantastic posture.

Sarah Parish

I've been fired five times for having a bad attitude.

Meg Rosoff

This generation... they have a different attitude. Instead of sitting and watching something, they want to be a part of it - they're very hedonistic and sensual.

Steve Wynn

My brother was a huge Charles Barkley fan - my brother went to Miami. He played power forward, and he always used to tell me stories about Barkley and college. And I watched Barkley growing up. I loved what he brought to the game. His toughness and just his attitude, being as strong he was.

Paul Pierce

There are actually no political aspirations. I think you need to have the right attitude and aptitude for it. I don't think I have the right aptitude for it. I think it is unfair to push somebody in that direction just because my father happens to be a politician.

Sonakshi Sinha

I perfectly understood President Obama's attitude throughout the French presidential campaign. He had no reason to distance himself from Nicolas Sarkozy. It's the basic solidarity that leaders who worked together owe to each other.

Francois Hollande

It's not too good to have this attitude in F1. It could be a disadvantage.

Alain Prost

I know there's millions of problems in the world, but if you dwell on those, then you're going to be miserable. I think my meditation helps me to transcend and get beyond the grip of all the negativity and regenerate from within a more positive attitude, which comes in very handy when you're going to do 150 concerts a year.

Mike Love

Not to discriminate every moment some passionate attitude in those about us, and in the very brilliancy of their gifts some tragic dividing on their ways, is, on this short day of frost and sun, to sleep before evening.

Walter Pater

Films for TV have to be much closer to the book, mainly because the objective with a TV movie that translates literature is to get the audience, after seeing this version, to pick up the book and read it themselves. My attitude is that TV can never really be any form of art, because it serves audience expectations.

Michael Haneke

With just about every player in Australia, his whole goal and ambition is to play for Australia. That's why they're playing first class cricket. It's just a different attitude.

Shane Warne

I think that the U.S. does have this very much more open attitude, and I admire it very much and I think it's very important to the world. But the information and the discussion sometimes come too late, after the effective decision has been made.

E. P. Thompson

Jazz in itself is not struggling. That is, the music itself is not struggling... It's the attitude that's in trouble. My plays insist that we should not forget or toss away our history.

August Wilson

I am always acting, be at a party, at work or in office. My attitude changes from meeting to meeting, from being serious to intense to funny, depending on who is in the room.

Karan Johar

Maybe it's just parenthood that puts you in a situation where you just have to develop a new attitude, I guess, about things.

James Mercer

I want to be in the big show, and to be in the big show, you have to practice. I have this attitude now that I'm going to take all the greatness I can. Nothing's going to stop me.

Steven Adler

I don't think people are fools, and I think they deserve a good attitude and smart entertainment.

Tatyana Tolstaya

It's really interesting with art-movies too, but art especially - to see how your attitude toward artists and works and your level of appreciation of them is always shifting and changing over the years.

Richard Hell

I know that, for me, I need to try to cover myself while breastfeeding so that no one snaps a picture. If this wasn't the case, I probably wouldn't mind as much because my son is my biggest concern. My attitude is, if someone sees a little somethin' somethin', don't look if you don't like it.

Kourtney Kardashian

Even when I'm playing someone named 'Fat Amy.' I'm all about confidence and attitude.

Rebel Wilson

To get nostalgic about other people's music, or even about your own, makes a terrible statement about the condition of your life and your prospects for the future. I have no patience with that kind of attitude, whether it's on radio or among friends.

Neil Peart

My attitude toward graduate students was different, I must say. I used graduate students as colleagues: I gave them the best problems to work on, and I encouraged them.

Frank Press

You'd like more people to recognise what you do is special. But I take the attitude that the best thing I can do for my sport is to be the best at it. The best way people will come to recognise that track and field is a great sport is to see athletes excelling at it. Which is what I intend to do.

Maurice Greene

When you Google me, you'll find a lot of people don't like Richard Dreyfuss. Because I'm cocky and I present a cocky attitude. But no one has ever disagreed with the notion I represent, that we need more civic education. So far there's 100 percent support for that.

Richard Dreyfuss

Our attitude is that we want to cross over. You can't go on making records just for your own hometown.

Cheryl James

I just think that people take me a little more seriously as a brunette. I don't know if that's just because of a societal preconceived notion that all blondes are stupid, but it's a different kind of attitude.

Kate Bosworth

It is impossible to exaggerate the wide, and widening, gulf between the American attitude on the Iraq war and the view from our friends across the Atlantic.

Nick Clooney

What do you mean by faith? Is faith enough for Man? Should he be satisfied with faith alone? Is there no way of finding out the truth? Is the attitude of faith, of believing in something for which there can be no more than philosophic proof, the true mark of a Christian?

Clifford D. Simak

I just really think every job I do, I get this gypsy attitude to money.

Jessica Brown Findlay

The music is first and foremost everything - no egos, no attitude, nothing - it's about the music.

Big Boi

Each experience through which we pass operates ultimately for our good. This is a correct attitude to adopt and we must be able to see it in that light.

Henry S. Haskins

I think Nina Simone has had an amazing journey. She was spicy and she had attitude and she didn't care, she wanted her money in a paper bag and don't mess with me and I've been doing some research on that so.

Nia Long

Donald Evans is a favorite person of mine. His worth ethic, his attitude and his dedication really set him apart.

Joe Greene

I utterly reject the view that the Third World is doomed to poverty and starvation. Not only is this wrong, I think this attitude verges on the immoral, like thinking that slavery is an unalterable facet of the human condition so why bother doing anything about it?

Alex Tabarrok

I totally let myself indulge, but I make little deals with myself. If I have an extra cupcake, I'll run a couple of extra miles. I think it's all about balance and not getting into extremes with dieting and exercising. Having a healthy attitude is important, too!

Megan Hilty

I have had it up to here with the prosecutions, the government's attitude, the judiciary, the media's stance and the majority of Turks who view the Kurdish people's justified cause through a nationalist lens.

Osman Baydemir

Getting into shape helped get me into a better mood, and when I'm in a better mood, I'm funnier. My general attitude is better.

Steve Howey

There are a lot of female artists my age around at the moment, but they're all American and blonde and blue-eyed and smiley. I'm totally the opposite of that. I want to show a bit more attitude and I have an opinion.

Samantha Mumba

For 'Fright Night,' we really want to convey the fun attitude of the movie and show the intensity of Colin Farrell as a predator. He's not a brooding vampire - he's dark and dangerous.

Stacey Snider

I think that, in the end, the military behavior and intelligence services are not very different from each other. It's an attitude of hunters; they're observing the prey.

Edgar Ramirez

Fame can be just so annoying because people are so critical of you. You can't just say, 'hi'. You say hi and people whisper' man did you see the way she said hi? What an attitude.

Juliette Lewis

I haven't seen Clones, which has been during this period when I haven't seen much of anything, but I did see Phantom Menace, and see my feelings about it - see, first of all, I think that when you make a lot of movies, your attitude about the movies changes.

Lawrence Kasdan

If the rights of civil partners are met differently in law to those of married couples, there is no discrimination in law, and if civil partnerships are seen as somehow 'second class' that is a social attitude which will change and cannot, in any case, be turned around by redefining the law of marriage.

John Sentamu

I like England more than I did when I left. It's become a bit of a better country in the last ten years, in the attitude of it. A bit more Americanized, which is both good and bad. At least when you order a cup of coffee they don't give you a hard time.

Teddy Thompson

A series of rumors about my attitude, as well as derogatory remarks about myself and my family showed me that the personal resentment of the Detroit general manager toward me would make it impossible for me to continue playing hockey in Detroit.

Ted Lindsay

The attitude of physiological psychology to sensations and feelings, considered as psychical elements, is, naturally, the attitude of psychology at large.

Wilhelm Wundt

A black suit can be classic and timeless and certainly for most occasions. But remember, it's not so much the color of suit as it is about the fit, cut, style, and, of course, attitude you have when wearing it.

John Varvatos

The money is in a different league these days, of course, but I have special memories of the 60s and 70s which players today don't have. There wasn't the same celebrity attitude and media exposure. We had a bit more freedom.

Peter Shilton

That attitude does not exist so much today, but in those days there was a very sharp distinction between basic physics and applied physics. Columbia did not deal with applied physics.

Gordon Gould

You'd like more people to recognise what you do is special. But I take the attitude that the best thing I can do for my sport is to be the best at it. The best way people will come to recognise that track and field is a great sport is to see athletes excelling at it.

Maurice Greene

Any time you have defensive ends going above you in the draft, when you know you put up numbers that were equal to better, you just have to use that as motivation. Whenever you're the underdog, you have to have the right attitude and just go out there and be yourself; just play.

Justin Tuck

I think it was my mom's attitude about art and being part of the narcissistic digital generation or whatever that made me think anyone would care what I had to say about anything!

Tavi Gevinson

Muslims have a very bad attitude to homosexuality, they're very intolerant.

Pim Fortuyn

Certain kinds of speed, flow, intensity, density of attacks, density of interaction... Music that concentrates on those qualities is, I think, easier achieved by free improvisation between people sharing a common attitude, a common language.

Evan Parker

My readers and my audiences have turned into my followers. They are more than interested in what I have to say in the subjects of sales, loyalty, attitude, networking, business social media, and becoming a trusted advisor.

Jeffrey Gitomer

I think to take your shirt off, you need to have a great body and more than that, confidence and attitude. It's all related. A great body equals confidence, and confidence equals attitude. And when you put all three together, you get a Salman Khan! And that's not me.

Riteish Deshmukh

I think we're in good hands. There's definitely much more momentum in bringing in good things to help support the show. Everyone's got a good attitude about it and I think that makes all the difference.

Crystal Chappell

Look, everything that you experience as a kid is the foundation of how you are today. I was brought up in a working class family in Leeds and when it comes to money both my parents worked hard and instilled the same attitude into me.

Melanie Brown

I like my hair long, and I love my bangs. I love them because I can pin them back or keep the fringe with attitude.

Cassie Steele

If I had been prime minister, I would have offered apologies to the Dutch Jewish community without hesitation. This would refer both to our government's attitude during the Second World War and to the very late postwar discovery that the restitution process had been poorly conceived.

Els Borst

Being sexy is all about attitude, not body type. It's a state of mind.

Amisha Patel

When I drank, I had a very different attitude towards my playing. It was sloppier but I kind of liked it that way. It was like the alcohol was telling my mind what to do.

Mick Mars

As Americans, we have traditionally been the optimists sporting the 'can-do' attitude. But when it comes to addressing climate adaptation and resiliency, we seem to be more 'can't do' than 'can-do.'

Paul Tonko

Measuring success in cultural diplomacy - the use of education, creative expression in any form, or people-to-people exchange to increase understanding across regions, cultures, or peoples - is challenging. How does one quantify changes in attitude, abandoning stereotypes, or feeling empathy as a result of a performance, a film, a book?

Cynthia P. Schneider

My father was a psychiatrist, the medical director of a mental hospital in Scotland, and when I was a student, I took vacation jobs there as a nursing assistant. So I did get to see mental illness, but I don't remember conversations about mental conditions. My father was a cheerful man with a robust attitude to such things.

Morag Joss

The compulsion to do good is an innate American trait. Only North Americans seem to believe that they always should, may, and actually can choose somebody with whom to share their blessings. Ultimately this attitude leads to bombing people into the acceptance of gifts.

Ivan Illich

A minister of Jesus Christ should not be regardless of his attitude. If he is the representative of Jesus Christ, his deportment, his attitude, his gestures, should be of that character which will not strike the beholder with disgust.

Ellen G. White

For a writer only one form of patriotism exists: his attitude toward language.

Joseph Brodsky

If you can kill animals, the same attitude can kill human beings. The mentality is the same which exploits nature and which creates wars.

Satish Kumar

Epic poetry exhibits life in some great symbolic attitude. It cannot strictly be said to symbolize life itself, but always some manner of life.

Lascelles Abercrombie

You can measure a programmer's perspective by noting his attitude on the continuing vitality of FORTRAN.

Alan Perlis

My father instilled in me the attitude of prevailing. If there's a challenge, go for it. If there's a wall to break down, break it down.

Donny Osmond

I failed the LSAT. Basically, if I had not failed, I'd have been a lawyer and there would be no Spanx. I think failure is nothing more than life's way of nudging you that you are off course. My attitude to failure is not attached to outcome, but in not trying. It is liberating.

Sara Blakely

France has been very good for me. It has given me a very worldly-cool attitude.

Marianne Faithfull

Right after 'Raymond' I had a world-is-my-oyster attitude, but I found out I don't like oysters. I had this existential emptiness. 'What is my purpose? Who am I?' I had a big identity crisis.

Ray Romano

Listen, whatever makes the movie better. That's the attitude you have to have.

Joseph Kosinski

I film quite a bit of footage, then edit. Changes before your eyes, things you can do and things you can't. My attitude is always 'let it keep rolling.'

Terrence Malick

Hollywood's a very weird place. I think there's less of everything except for attitude.

Dean Cain

When I was in my 20s it did occur to me that there was something perverted about an attitude that thought that killing somebody was a minor offence compared to kissing somebody.

John McGahern

When you are facing the wilderness on your own, you have a totally different attitude to someone who works in government or who has a monthly cheque.

Rick Santelli

Canadians tend to be a bit more religious than most Europeans - though not more than the Poles or Ukrainians. Most important, their attitude to immigration and ethnic minorities is more positive than that of most Europeans.

Timothy Garton Ash

One day I looked in the mirror, and I wasn't happy. If you're not feeling good mentally, emotionally and physically, you're just a mess - and that's the point I felt like. It was a change in attitude and a shift in lifestyle. There's no crazy diet; I train six days a week, and I eat really well.

Ricki-Lee Coulter

I'm allergic to attitude.

Megan Boone

I came on to the film with a very happy-go-lucky attitude which I think my character, Charlie, did when she went into the house. I expected it to be good, and then slowly things started to change for us all.

Jennifer Sky

Refuse to be a lazy Christian, and resist a passive, apathetic attitude.

Joyce Meyer

I walk tall; I got a tall attitude.

Dolly Parton

If I had been asked to write 1,200 words for a newspaper tomorrow, on any subject, I would just do it rather than leave a white hole in the page. And I think it's a very healthy attitude to take to writing anything.

Tom Stoppard

I do believe that during the Bush-Cheney administration, that Vice President Cheney set a tone and an attitude for the CIA.

Nancy Pelosi

The attitude of the Democrat Party is that wherever there are Republicans they are so bad, they are so discriminatory, they are so racist, they're so bigoted, they're just such reprobates that we can't afford to let them have any say whatsoever in what's happening.

Rush Limbaugh

Obama does not represent America. Nor does he represent anything what our forefathers stood for. This country is basically built on an attitude. It's a way of life. It's not because you're born here. It's not that you're supposed to take from those who have and give to those who haven't. That kills a country. It killed Russia.

Luke Scott

When I go to the clinic next and sit with a tube in my arm and watch the poison go in, I'm in an attitude of abject passivity. It doesn't feel like fighting at all; it just feels like submitting.

Christopher Hitchens

My attitude is, do as much as I can while I'm free. And if I'm arrested I'll still do as much as I can.

Aung San Suu Kyi

Americans are the most generous country on the planet. I've worked in Europe, I've worked in Australia. There is no where else where you get absolutely no attitude for being a foreigner. If you do your job well, they embrace you.

Hugh Jackman

I developed a nutty attitude where I'd think, If some guy really loves me he doesn't care if I'm fat. I'd come up with all these stupid reasons why it would be OK to be fat.

Kirstie Alley

Over the years, I've become barraged by comments from people, such as, 'Beam me up, Scotty!' and I became defensive. I felt they were derisive and engendered an attitude. I am grateful for the success, but didn't want to be mocked.

William Shatner

I've never run into a guy who could win at the top level in anything today and didn't have the right attitude, didn't give it everything he had, at least while he was doing it; wasn't prepared and didn't have the whole program worked out.

Ted Turner

I was impressed by Hendrix. Not so much by his playing, as his attitude - he wasn't a great player, but everything else about him was brilliant.

Ritchie Blackmore

My attitude when I'm in Mexico is I wake up in the morning with nothing to do and I go to bed half done. I don't wear a watch. When I live down there, I do nothing according to time. I eat when I'm hungry and go to sleep when I'm tired.

Jesse Ventura

I love women with attitude.

Kevin Hart

People think, 'She's a model. She must have such an attitude. She must be so stuck up.' But I'm normal. I cry. I'm not rich. I drive a 1987 Chevrolet Celebrity.

Summer Altice

I am very surprised by someone like Alexander Wang. I am amazed how he is good with fashion, with business, with public relations himself, with an attitude in his clothes that is spoken immediately.

Carine Roitfeld

It was just like a dream. I could have ended up with an album that's not all that different from anything else coming out of Nashville. Mutt made the difference. He took these songs, my attitude, my creativity, and colored them in a way that is unique.

Shania Twain

When I first started writing songs and being very explicit, it was hard, but one of the main things people respond to in my writing is that 'just say it' attitude of my songs. There really is nothing personal or private; it's all universal, if you can just find the courage to be open about your life.

Ani DiFranco

When you retire, it's a place in life, a part of the journey. You just don't quit work; you develop an attitude where you can do what you please.

Tom T. Hall

The idea of politics is just so uninteresting to me - I've never paid much attention to it. I don't believe things can really change. It doesn't matter who's president. Nothing really gets resolved. I don't know. I guess that's not the right attitude to take.

Trent Reznor

Religion has nothing to do with God. It's a fundamental attitude of human beings, who ask about the origins of life and what happens after death. For many, the answer is a personal god. In my opinion, it's religion that produces God, not the other way round.

Umberto Eco

I like to help kids, work with kids in detention homes. Don't tell a kid what's right and wrong. He knows what's right and wrong. Find out what his attitude and his aptitude are; try to help him where he wants to go.

Evel Knievel

On 'Van Halen,' I was a young punk, and everything revolved around the fastest kid in town, gunslinger attitude. But I'd say that at the time of 'Fair Warning,' I started concentrating more on songwriting. But I guess in most people's minds I'm just a gunslinger.

Eddie Van Halen

There is clearly a constituency that appreciates the message that Google is sending, that it finds the Chinese government's attitude to the Internet and censorship unacceptable.

Rebecca MacKinnon

Have you seen some of the women - and the men - in Los Angeles? They pay surgeons to make them look completely different in the hope of finding their youth. But youth comes from within. If you have a young attitude, then that can show in your face, the way you walk and move.

Kim Cattrall

It's a question of keeping one's eyes and ears open and watching how other people play the game. They're watching me too, to see what my attitude is like.

Charles Dance

It's not the style that motivates me, as much as an attitude of openness that I have when I go into a project.

Herbie Hancock

The characteristic political attitude of today is not one of positive belief, but of despair.

Herbert Read

The attitude we have towards our personal pets as opposed to the animals that suffer under the factory farm is hypocritical and delusional.

James Cromwell

In just the same way the thousands of successive positions of a runner are contracted into one sole symbolic attitude, which our eye perceives, which art reproduces, and which becomes for everyone the image of a man who runs.

Henri Bergson

I don't mean this in a stuck-up way, but I needed an attitude song.

Gwen Stefani

The accounting of the sacrifice is, more than anything else, the attitude toward war memorials in our time.

Friedrich St. Florian

There is an attitude that we should be able to have everything. No, you shouldn't be able to have anything. I'd like a helicopter, but I can't afford a helicopter, so I don't buy one. People are buying stuff they can't afford on credit. I bought my Ford hybrid with cash.

Grace Slick

I met my grandfather just before he died, and it was the first time that I had seen Dad with a relative of his. It was interesting to see my own father as a son and the body language and alteration in attitude that comes with that, and it sort of changed our relationship for the better.

Christian Bale

I can remember that on the shelves at home, there were these books by Thomas Wolfe. 'Look Homeward Angel' and 'Of

Time and the River.' 'Of Time and the River' had just come out when I was aware of his name. My parents had a hard time convincing me that he was no kin whatsoever. My attitude was, 'Well, what's he doing on the shelf, then?'

Tom Wolfe

I really believe you can predict when someone has a great attitude, a real well of talent.

Taylor Hackford

You can't beat the beehive for glam punkette attitude.

Rob Sheffield

An American orchestra doesn't want to play more than it has to. I respectfully disagree with that attitude.

Zubin Mehta

Today, I think the attitude is that governing is not necessarily good politics, and the result is that it's much more partisan and much more divided.

Leon Panetta

With all due respect to Mick Jagger, who is one of my idols, I think it's a mistake to leap around and sing at 53. When I started, there weren't any women I looked up to. It was Mick. I never saw anybody go on a stage and have that tongue-in-cheek attitude. It was all straight, including the Beatles. I love his attitude, hands on hips and lips out.

Grace Slick

If philosophy is practice, a demand to know the manner in which its history is to be studied is entailed: a theoretical attitude toward it becomes real only in the living appropriation of its contents from the texts.

Karl Jaspers

If you can attribute your success entirely to your own mental effort, to your own attitude, to some spiritual essence that you have that is better than other people's, then that must feel pretty good.

Barbara Ehrenreich

Let us change our traditional attitude to the construction of programs. Instead of imagining that our main task is to instruct a computer what to do, let us concentrate rather on explaining to human beings what we want a computer to do.

Donald Knuth

This is the paradox for me: in failure alone is there any possibility of success. I don't think I'm alone in this - nor do I think it's an attitude that only prevails among people whose work is obviously 'creative'.

Will Self

No one's going to be able to operate without a grounding in the basic sciences. Language would be helpful, although English is becoming increasingly international. And travel. You have to have a global attitude.

Rupert Murdoch

Oh, I don't think Tom Sowell would tell anybody to join the administration. That's not his style. But I think his attitude has always been if it had to be done he'd prefer me to do it than somebody else.

Clarence Thomas

But I think bands that rolled in with a big attitude, like they were some big deal, I just found that very strange.

Rob Zombie

I trained as a journalist in America where paying sources is frowned upon. Now I work in the U.K. where there is a more flexible attitude.

Heather Brooke

Music is the way I understand how to communicate now, the way that I've learned how to communicate... but it will eventually have to go beyond that. You see, I've realised that music is not what keeps people involved - it's the attitude behind the music.

Todd Rundgren

Part of the punk attitude was that you should project your music through your whole body... show your personality as much as possible.

Billy Idol

I may not be the number one movie star, or my films might not be doing too good. I am grateful for what life has offered me. I have got a great family, parents are together, have a great sister, I get to holiday. All these things make me grateful towards life, for everything. I always say - have an attitude of gratitude.

Sonam Kapoor

In regard to music, I just think that it's always best to have an attitude of being a perpetual student and always look to learn something new about music, because there's always something new to learn.

David Sanborn

You can't be a crazy rebel in the face of death, it's not a fitting attitude.

Michel Houellebecq

My attitude to writing is like when you do wallpapering, you remember where all the little bits are that don't meet. And then your friends say: It's terrific!

Harrison Birtwistle

I just try to try to keep an attitude that I don't know what I'm doing. Not to the point where I'm beating myself up, but I just go in thinking that I have a lot to learn. And I hope I still have that attitude 30 years from now.

Tobey Maguire

The phenomenon of home schooling is a wonderful example of the American can-do attitude. Growing numbers of parents have become disenchanted with government-run public schools. Many parents have simply taken matters into their own hands, literally.

Steve Forbes

I think my attitude to human beings has changed since leaving prison.

Jeffrey Archer

In the West, you have always associated the Islamic faith 100 percent with Arab culture. This in itself is a fundamentalist attitude and it is mistaken.

Youssou N'Dour

The place of chess in the society is closely related to the attitude of young people towards our game.

Boris Spassky

Along with its enchanting and exquisite melodies, West Side Story has attitude and a tremendous amount of frenetic energy. It's emotional, theatrical and technical. It's everything.

Steve Vai

Reason is an action of the mind; knowledge is a possession of the mind; but faith is an attitude of the person. It means you are prepared to stake yourself on something being so.

Michael Ramsey

The reality is I'm not this person with this driving 'get it done' attitude.

Greg Giraldo

I can't believe the pro-choicers attitude toward unborn children-to me it's the ultimate liberal cause, to defend those without a voice.

Michael Aston

There has been a change in attitude, though.

Daniel Petrie

Elvis Costello had a brand new bag. He was a musician, but he knew all about the attitude part of it.

Nick Lowe

Americans have always had an ambivalent attitude toward intelligence. When they feel threatened, they want a lot of it, and when they don't, they regard the whole thing as somewhat immoral.

Vernon A. Walters

I need that aggressive attitude to play my music and more men have that attitude than women.

Lita Ford

I'm not a music lover in the sense that I look for something to have on. I've never had that attitude to music.

Harrison Birtwistle

For me, personally, life in South Africa had come to an end. I had been lucky in some of the whites I had met. Meeting them had made a straight 'all-blacks-are-good, all-whites-are-bad' attitude impossible. But I had reached a point where the gestures of even my friends among the whites were suspect, so I had to go or be forever lost.

Peter Abrahams

What reader wants to be told what attitude to strike?

Ian Mcewan

Lead singers not only do the majority of the work, but their personalities are singled out and taken as the general attitude of the unit.

Martha Reeves

We have all met people that act 'old' or think a number makes them old, and I truly don't believe that is the case. If you have a good attitude toward aging, and you do what you can to live healthy and take care of yourself, I don't think the number matters.

Tabatha Coffey

So at a time in which the media give the public everything it wants and desires, maybe art should adopt a much more aggressive attitude towards the public. I myself am very much inclined to take this position.

Thom Mayne

I still have a young attitude.

Pat Morita

Women didn't want to be on the stage with other women because they didn't want their bodies to be compared. They didn't want another female act opening for them because of this weird competitive and tokenistic attitude.

Kathleen Hanna

Before the sacred, people lose all sense of power and all confidence; they occupy a powerless and humble attitude toward it. And yet no thing is sacred of itself, but by my declaring it sacred, by my declaration, my judgment, my bending the knee; in short, by my - conscience.

Max Stirner

I was always spiritual, even as a child. I was taught to pray, show gratitude. We had an attitude of gratitude. Even if life was ugly, bad or sad - we prayed.

Shilpa Shetty

In some way, people believe that if you are permeable, if you are a good listener, you don't have the quality of somebody with a firm attitude. This is what, fundamentally, I got from my mother.

Renzo Piano

The traditional Christian attitude toward human personality was that human nature was essentially good and that it was formed and modified by social pressures and training.

Carroll Quigley

I think my attitude has always been to put food on the table.

James Garner

I am a Piscean, and they have a lovingly detached attitude towards life.

Shahid Kapoor

In aid, the proper attitude is one omitting gratitude.

Marya Mannes

Having a child makes you strong and gives you chutzpah. It relaxed my attitude to the job; my center of focus shifted, which I think is very helpful, because even if you're not a very indulgent actor you spend a lot of time thinking about yourself. I don't think that is particularly healthy.

Imelda Staunton

My parents have a strong work ethic, but their attitude to life, their philosophy, is: 'whatever makes you happy.'

Sally Hawkins

I want to read about a character doing something fairly quiet where I can picture who the character is, and what their attitude towards the world is - which I'm a lot more interested in than what they do under the pressure of a gunfight.

Samuel R. Delany

Any time I need to get a serious attitude adjustment, I put on one of their records, and there are examples there for all time to keep us honest and keep us reaching; they'll never be eclipsed.

Benny Green

We have become aware of the responsibility for our attitude towards the dark pages in our history. We have understood that bad service is done to the nation by those who are impelling to renounce that past.

Aleksander Kwasniewski

I don't reflect much, unless I'm talking to the media. I have more of a 'Forward, march!' kind of attitude.

Kerry King

I was entirely natural and in many ways I have the same attitude now. I don't mourn the loss of my youth because I believe you should enjoy what you have while you have it.

Koo Stark

Before the sacred, people lost all sense of power and all confidence; they occupy a powerless and humble attitude toward it. And yet no thing is sacred of itself, but by declaring it sacred, by my declaration, my judgment, my bending the knee; in short, by my - conscience.

Max Stirner

I think the truth is, we are all racist, really, when it comes down to it. I think all of us have to check ourselves from time to time, and say, 'Look, that sort of attitude isn't good enough.' It takes discipline to keep our prejudices out.

Peter Hollingworth

Hardboiled crime fiction came of age in 'Black Mask' magazine during the Twenties and Thirties. Writers like Dashiell Hammett and Raymond Chandler learnt their craft and developed a distinct literary style and attitude toward the modern world.

Charles Frazier

Tommie Aaron taught me how to have a good attitude, to be easy going and not get uptight.

Dale Murphy

I couldn't go now to a brand that had a niche attitude like... gothic. I couldn't do that. Well, I could do it, but I wouldn't find it interesting, challenging.

Raf Simons

I'm going to try to enjoy the All-Star break, hope my players reflect on what happened the first half of the season, come back with a different attitude, try to find our solution on how to win it.

Don Baylor

You can learn what you want to learn through hard work. And a good employer will teach you what you want to learn as long as you show the right attitude and behaviors.

Gerald Chertavian

While I put forth the suntan and the teeth and the cavalier attitude, I've survived under the worst of eras and times, and I've always had a good time doing it, because I never really took myself seriously, nor did I take life seriously because it is already terribly serious.

George Hamilton

Everyone has attitude, and I think everyone should have attitude. But I know I have attitude, but that's just, I think if you don't have attitude, it comes only with self confidence. So if you don't have self confidence, you won't have attitude, and I think there's a difference when you have attitude and when you have arrogance.

Sania Mirza

The problem was just a mean attitude that festers and has to be challenged.

Major Owens

As I wrote, I found that Aibileen had some things to say that really weren't in her character. She was older, soft-spoken, and she started showing some attitude.

Kathryn Stockett

I just want to go in with the right attitude and from Day 1 make a difference.

Freddy Adu

Our new attitude is how can we put you in front of our customer.

Terry Semel

A discipline I have observed is an attitude of love and reverence to people.

Bessie Head

Social mores change all the time. In the mid-1970s, it would've been astonishing, say, to see two men holding hands in the streets. And the attitude to having a fling with a girl, or whatever, was quite different then.

Robert Harris

But having said that, there's also a sea change in attitude towards media.

Robert McChesney

My dad instilled in me a great sense of humor. I wasn't bullied at school because my outward attitude was confident, and that helps.

Warwick Davis

Every story I write adds to me a little, changes me a little, forces me to reexamine an attitude or belief, causes me to research and learn, helps me to understand people and grow.

Octavia E. Butler

I came back to performing with a different attitude about performing and myself. I wasn't expecting perfection any more, just hoping for an occasional inspiration.

Neil Diamond

In 1977, at least, he wished to have people believe that he shared and was proud of an attitude toward women that is not acceptable in a politician. In 2003, all he has said is that he doesn't remember the interview.

Michael Kinsley

I'm a big fan of Courtney Love. I love Hole and I love her acting and I love her attitude. I just hope I never meet her in a dark alley.

Jeff Ross

My opponents attitude is, 'If it moves, tax it, if it keeps moving, regulate it and when it stops, subsidize it.

Rob Simmons

I don't know that I have any role models now that are fixed. Definitely my mom - she's the coolest. She's worked really hard her whole life and I just think she's got a great attitude. Moms just know so much it's so silly.

Larisa Oleynik

What a stupid attitude we have in this country to personal stories.

Amanda Burton

My attitude about Hollywood is that I wouldn't walk across the street to pull one of those executives out of the snow if he was bleeding to death. Not unless I was paid for it. None of them ever did me any favors.

James Woods

The world is full of musicians who can play great, and you wouldn't cross the road to see them. It's people who have this indefinable attitude that are the good ones.

Nick Lowe

It's true, some senior Hungarian writers are not known for their laughter. There is a strong Germanic influence - an attitude that if it's enjoyable it can't possibly be literature.

Tibor Fischer

I like actors that are good with pantomime and that can transmit a lot by their presence and attitude more than through their dialogue.

Guillermo del Toro

The Olympic Games are a national cause, and a national cause calls for a nationwide attitude.

Gianna Angelopoulos-Daskalaki

Somehow, the greater the public opposition to the health care bill, the more determined they seem to force it on us anyway. Their attitude shows Washington at its very worst - the presumption that they know best, and they're going to get their way whether the American people like it or not.

Scott Brown

After working for years in Hollywood where the actors have taken over, it was a real relief to get down there and not only have some children, but also have some actors that had no attitude.

Phillip Noyce

There's a punk-rock attitude, clearly, to 'Hated.' There's even a punk-rock attitude to 'The Hangover,' I think. We start the movie with a Glenn Danzig song.

Todd Phillips

A Maybelline New York woman is strong and confident - I love that attitude.

Frida Gustavsson

The war changed everybody's attitude. We became international almost overnight.

W. Averell Harriman

My grandmother is this amazingly theatrical woman. She acted like a movie star, as far as looks and attitude, kind of like Susan Hayward.

Parker Posey

There is something so biologically implausible that your attitude is going to cure a disease. There's a tremendous arrogance to imagine that your mind is all that powerful.

Marcia Angell

I liked painting and drawing, and I liked humanities mainly - poetry, literature - this speculative attitude toward life.

Rafael Moneo

I think it has other roots, has to do, in part, with a general anxiety in contemporary life... nuclear bombs, inequality of possibility and chance, inequality of goods allotted to us, a kind of general racist, unjust attitude that is pervasive.

Leonard Baskin

If I don't make the team out of spring training, I'll keep a good attitude. I'll just go polish up the parts of my game that made me not stay in the big leagues.

Cory Lidle

I always had the attitude that I wanted to throw a no-hitter every game.

Dennis Eckersley

I don't return anybody's calls unless it's going to mean extra money for me. And I've completely cut off all relationships with any friends that I had before the show. And I've copped an attitude.

Mike Judge

Unfortunately, the attitude of many towards the press, humanitarians included and especially government workers, is often one of suspicion, if not outright fear.

Alvin Adams

Livelihoods and whole communities throughout the Murray-Darling Basin have been imperilled by the workings of drought, fire, flood, acid mud and human action over many decades. In the rescues and the cleanups and the long hauls, I see the same attitude over and again. People just rally and get on with it.

Quentin Bryce

I always have one or two, sometimes more, Navajo or other tribes' cultural elements in mind when I start a plot. In Thief of Time, I wanted to make readers aware of Navajo attitude toward the dead, respect for burial sites.

Tony Hillerman

I have had the view that cutting wages is not the path to prosperity, and one of the great myths propagated about my attitude to industrial relations is that I believe in lower wages. I've never believed in lower wages. Never. Never believed in lower wages, I've never believed in lower wages as an economic instrument.

John Howard

I will not get very far with this attitude.

Nancy Cartwright

Just because you're a luxury brand doesn't mean you have to have an attitude.

Angela Ahrendts

I try and have a relaxed attitude and stay quite switched off until about an hour before kick-off.

Roy Keane

Football is my profession now. I'm getting married in August...
It's a new experience for me as someone just getting out of
college. I still have the same attitude about football I always
had. I play hard. I enjoy practice. I'd rather be throwing in
passing drills than sitting around and watching TV.

Doug Flutie

To so enter into it in nature and art that the enjoyed meanings
of life may become a part of living is the attitude of aesthetic
appreciation.

George Herbert Mead

You've got to leave the reader with more than just a name and
a costume - they need to know who the character is, what
they're like, what kind of attitude they have, what sort of role
they play.

Kurt Busiek

Even with, or perhaps, because of, this background, I have
over the past few years sensed a very dramatic change in
attitude on the part of Prince Edward Islanders towards the ongoing rush for so-called modernization.

Alex Campbell

I thought I was going to be killed. The casualties were so heavy, it was just a given. I learned to take each day, each mission, as it came. That's an attitude I've carried into my professional life. I take each case, each job, as it comes.

Elliot Richardson

Here you do have forests, where pigs could be raised by letting them root about in the forests for a good part of the year. Therefore, you have a different attitude toward them compared with what continues to exist in the Middle East.

Marvin Harris

For something to be useful to the spirit is not very valuable to get your covered wagon across the desert. We have adopted that attitude so thoroughly that any American father whose son tells him he wants to write poetry will be embarrassed.

Miller Williams

I grew up in a rough environment. You want to be strong and have your presence felt out there. That attitude reflects how people see you.

Mekhi Phifer

What I wish I had, is that I wish I was a little more Greek, in that I wish I could lose my North American driven attitude and that I could be a little bit more poetic and laissez faire.

Nia Vardalos

As a team, you need to come from behind every once in awhile just to do it. Good for the attitude. It makes it exciting. And when everybody knows you have to throw it... that makes it fun too.

Dan Marino

In Scotland over many years we have cultivated through our justice system what I hope can be described as a 'culture of compassion.' On the other hand, there still exists in many parts of the U.S., if not nationally, an attitude towards the concept of justice which can only be described as a 'culture of vengeance.'

Keith O'Brien

It's tricky. I've never been standing at the top of the tree with tons of money thrown at me. I've never really had a profile. So in a way I have this 'nothing to lose' attitude.

Joel Edgerton

The American attitude is 'We're the best'. That's why the NBA guys who come from other countries, the Europeans, all sort of stick together away from the game.

Andrew Bogut

There is no planning. On the night it is really great, it's euphoria and if it is not so great there is always tomorrow night. That was his attitude.

Ed McMahon

Like our attitude to love, truth and goodness, we seem to be confident about knowing what beauty is - certain, even dogmatic - until we think hard about the idea, whereupon all confidence flies away.

Charles Jencks

You walk into the playgrounds in Shanghai and Beijing, and you see youngsters who are shorter, shaking and baking and having attitude. And Jeremy Lin is going to inspire all of them.

David Stern

The artist is not responsible to any one. His social role is asocial... his only responsibility consists in an attitude to the work he does.

Georg Baselitz

I think leather pants are just better than jeans onstage; they give the performance a nice attitude, and they are also shockingly comfortable. Comfort is key.

Jessie Baylin

We will see that our new attitude toward liquor has been given to us without any thought or effort on our part. It just comes! That is the miracle of it.

William Griffith Wilson

This hook nose and crab meister attitude has gotten me every job I've ever had. And more divorces than I care to remember.

Norman Fell

The U.S. tries to provide immigrants who grow up here with a world-class education and imbue them with the can-do attitude that has long defined American innovation.

Gary Locke

I've always been a guy who's pretty supportive, its just my nature, so I came in to the situation with the attitude that I wanted to support Johnny and make it work.

Rick Derringer

There's a certain attitude to Los Angeles.

Inara George

I also had a mistaken attitude towards certain comrades.

Bela Kun

I think every role you get is going to be a powerful one. As long as you go in with the mindset of, 'Yeah, I'm going to make the most of this.' So that's the kind of attitude I take into each role that I play.

Anna Hutchison

Our spiritual attitude is determined by our conception of our relation to infinite spirit.

Paul Twitchell

Athletic competition clearly defines the unique power of our attitude.

Bart Starr

If you take the contempt some Americans have for yuppies and multiply it by 10 you might come close to understanding their attitude towards the City, as they call it - London, the people of the south.

Martin Cruz Smith

I haven't watched 'Mad TV' a lot, but I have seen some stuff on there that is truly funny. You have to have some sort of attitude toward the subject, and they seem to have it. It depends on how much blood you want to draw.

Joe Flaherty

There is a very deep conviction in the heart of the people who work in al-Jazeera that if it changes its editorial line, it will very quickly lose its audience. Al-Jazeera has its own style; it has more than 3,500 employees, and I don't think anyone will have the attitude of changing it because they will lose.

Wadah Khanfar

For me, music is all about emotion and attitude.

Peter Criss

If wearing the Spanx helps you get looks, and you feel that energy and response, and you're rocking your body with confidence, that's still how you'll feel about yourself when you get home and take the Spanx off... If your attitude improves from the Spanx, wear the Spanx!

Lisa Ann Walter

Turkey wants a policy of engagement exactly like President Obama's new approach. Policy of engagement, less confrontation, less tense attitude, especially in the region.

Ahmet Davutoglu

Sid Vicious began the age of participation in which everyone could be the artist. Sid proved that you don't have to play well to be the star. You can play badly, or not even at all. I endorsed that attitude. If you can't write songs, no problem - simply steal one and change it to your taste.

Malcolm Mclaren

The townspeople outside the reservations had a very superior attitude toward Indians, which was kind of funny, because they weren't very wealthy; they were on the fringes of society themselves.

James Welch

I know a lot of Eastern Europeans, and because of what they have been through and what they have seen, they have an attitude where they are not easily fooled.

Francine Prose

I like looking at the characters. Seeing them always brings up some voice or attitude. I am much more visual, and that works so much better than having someone tell me what the character is all about.

Frank Welker

I've done a lot of movies that don't have any music in them, and I've always sort of had a kind of wary attitude about music because it can be so manipulative, and also because with pop music, I feel like everybody kind of has their own relationship to songs.

Joe Swanberg

I love a woman in a tuxedo, or in a dress, who looks comfortable, relaxed, happy. I'd love to dress Daphne Guinness - she has exactly that attitude.

Stephane Rolland

I love a woman with a relaxed attitude.

Stephane Rolland

I had an attitude problem when I was a kid. I'm not gonna lie.

Tionne Watkins

I have the same attitude with work - I like to go to work, I like to work really hard I, like to give everything my all, I like to try things that are new, you know.

Rosie Huntington-Whiteley

Its attitude, which it has preached and practiced, is skepticism. Now, it finds, the public is applying that skepticism to the press.

Thomas Griffith

Patton was living in the Dark Ages. Soldiers were peasants to him. I didn't like that attitude.

Bill Mauldin

If I or any other black can deliver at the box office, I'll get a lot of work. Too many young actors, regardless of their color, try to play an attitude on camera and fail to remember their job is to fit into an entertainment.

Mario Van Peebles

Bader's philosophy was my philosophy. His whole attitude to life was mine.

Kenneth More

The attitude of the actor is his interpretation of what he reads, and the written word is what creates the role in the actor's mind, and I guess in reading the things that were given to me, I reacted as you guys saw me, you know.

Gene Barry

First, I was so dazzled and besotted by India. People said the poverty was biblical, and I'm afraid that was my attitude, too. It's terribly easy to get used to someone else's poverty if you're living a middle-class life in it. But after a while, I saw it wasn't possible to accept it, and I also didn't want to.

Ruth Prawer Jhabvala

I'd like to get out of Philadelphia. I don't care for the people or their attitude, although they don't bother me or my play. But maybe the Phillies can get a couple of broken bats and shower shoes for me.

Richie Allen

When I speak in English, my expressions become different. My attitude, too. I'm not sure why, but there really is a difference. My hands move differently when I speak English.

Gong Li

You know, who cares about seeing the girls when everybody wants to see the band. That's what's important, KISS is important. I think we look great, and the attitude is there, and I'm real happy with it.

Eric Carr

People kind of have a misconception, because when someone calls me Theo and I correct them, say, 'No, my name is Malcolm,' they think I have an attitude about it and I don't want to be associated with the show.

Malcolm-Jamal Warner

Sexy is attitude, but fitness for me is my dance. I dance two hours nearly every day. You break into good sweat, and it doesn't even feel like exercise. Apart from that, I enjoy Pilates.

Jiah Khan

People's attitude seems to be that if you don't have a television, you're not connected to reality - somehow you're not in reality. It's quite interesting, because I suspect that possibly it's the reverse.

Jodhi May

My first feeling about the paper and the attitude is that it is absurd.

Arthur Holly Compton

The attitude of the people proves that not only do we want to, but that we can succeed in pulling our country out of the difficult position it finds itself in. The banking system of our country will survive and grow.

Nicos Anastasiades

It can be easy to buy into anything. I would lose focus if I went with that attitude of wanting to be famous.

Tristan MacManus

I've spent a lot of time in L.A. and I love it. A lot of Brits can't stand the place, but I like the West Coast attitude and the way people celebrate success.

Sophia Myles

I always wanted to be a filmmaker, but I started acting when I was 9 years old. I looked a certain part that I wasn't, really. I played, you know, a high school jock with a lot of attitude or a spoiled rich kid, and I was neither of those things. I was from a very working-class family in Van Nuys.

Steve Antin

I think 'Gatsby' is hobbled, in part, by its status as a Great American Novel. People kind of roll their eyes before they've even opened it, treat it with a 'been there, done that' attitude. I know I did. It took me years to re-open the novel and see how much I'd missed.

Susan Choi

You have to have an attitude that nothing's gonna stop me. I think that's just my New York kind of attitude - survival of the fittest.

Melissa De Sousa

My father got a trade union scholarship to Oxford; he lived and breathed politics; he was always watching current-affairs programmes. But I have a five-year-old child's attitude towards the news. Mainly, that it absolutely turns me off.

Jez Butterworth

I've never been in any country for more than four years, and I'm learning different languages all the time. It gives you a different attitude.

Santiago Cabrera

My heroes, I couldn't imagine them practicing. Like Bob Dylan, you know? Bob Dylan's a very, very good guitar player, but it's like he's trying to hide it. I always loved this attitude. When you're very good... it's like being an athlete - and I always hated sports!

Laurent Brancowitz

I have met so many people who are negative, and it tells on their attitude towards life and towards everything.

Phaneesh Murthy

I'm ephemeral as much as I can be, so I started to think about the idea of not working. It's really about a change of attitude. It's not so much about stopping, but about re-thinking the meaning of one's production.

Rirkrit Tiravanija

Going back and forth between Western Arabic and African countries clearly created the various musical backgrounds I could have and obviously influenced my professional attitude, my way of approaching both music composition and singing, particularly phrasing.

Rokia Traore

What I learned with tech companies is I gotta give people room to experiment, and also to make what might later on be a mistake. This is the attitude I want to build within San Francisco - give some time to the tech community.

Ed Lee

What really went wrong is that General Motors has had this philosophy from the beginning that what's good for General Motors is good for the country. So, their attitude was, 'We'll build it and you buy it. We'll tell you what to buy. You just buy it.'

Michael Moore

I cannot say that the attitude of the United Nations always is for the Israeli attitude. Israel, I think, has been under severe attacks by members of the United Nations many times.

Ariel Sharon

Design is about point of view, and there should be some sort of woman or lifestyle or attitude in one's head as a designer. So my being able to reach the masses was something that meant a great deal to me - especially for women who could never wear Vera Wang.

Vera Wang

The Senator from Massachusetts has given us ample grounds to doubt the judgment and the attitude he brings to bear on vital issues of national security.

Dick Cheney

America won the Cold War by protecting our strategic resources from the threat of foreign control. We must bring the same attitude to our trade relationship with China.

Jo Ann Emerson

My personal view is that such total planning by the state is an absolute good and not simply a relative good... I do not myself think of the attitude I take as deriving from Marx - though this undoubtedly will be suggested - but from Fichte and Hegel.

John Grierson

Beyonce is one of my inspirations. Her attitude, her style, her voice... she's perfect.

Charice Pempengco

I didn't really know what to expect, but I thought there aren't a lot of rap groups that can say they have a documentary done about them, so my attitude was like, 'Shoot, why not?' I'm sure there are a lot of people that would like to take our place. I felt like we should all embrace it.

Phife Dawg

Global political conditions make a direct American intervention difficult, but President Reagan's messianic and visceral attitude toward the Nicaraguan revolution could mean it will happen as an act of desperation.

Tomas Borge

My attitude toward men who mess around is simple: If you find 'em, kill 'em.

Loretta Lynn

I didn't know how to show my self love, and I didn't want anyone else to hurt me. So my tough girl attitude was like, 'I'm not having it.'

Mary J. Blige

You lose attitude when you feel too comfortable, so I prefer to wear clothes that have a certain edge to them.

Carine Roitfeld

I certainly don't disparage someone whose attitude towards their work is utterly different from mine - that's up to them.

Ian Mckellen

As a life coach, I love makeovers, from new clothes to surgery, pedicures to highlights. But redoing makes you feel better only if approached with the right attitude.

Martha Beck

Britishness is just a way of putting things together and a certain don't care attitude about clothes. You don't care, you just do it and it looks great.

Vivienne Westwood

I think it has something to do with being British. We don't take ourselves as seriously as some other countries do. I think a lot of people take themselves far too seriously; I find that a very tedious attitude.

Joan Collins

The single biggest surprise about arriving to the Senate is the defeatist attitude here.

Ted Cruz

Some actors specialize in shooting weapons and punching people. Some have the market on playing buffoons cornered, others specialize in roles that require heavy makeup or outrageous wardrobe. Some trade exclusively in a post-ironic blase attitude.

Rob Lowe

I can pull off anything; I have the height and the attitude. The only thing I can't wear is a leotard, but I can wear anything else.

Theophilus London

I remember early on, in my very, very early days, I had a makeup artist tell me that I needed to get an attitude. I had no idea what he was talking about.

Andie MacDowell

I have a very childish attitude to books - a very non-analytic enthusiasm... like Alice falling down the chute.

Mariella Frostrup

I'm taking a bit of a wait-and-see attitude towards 3D.

Christopher Nolan

The attitude is we live and let live. This is actually an amazing change in values in a rather short time and it's an example of freedom from religion.

Tom Wolfe

Part of our western outlook stems from the scientific attitude and its method of isolating the parts of a phenomenon in order to analyze them.

Arthur Erickson

Iraq is just a symbol of the attitude of western democracies to the rest of the world.

Harold Pinter

I think the attraction of 'American Idol' is about the basic human nature attitude that is, 'We can put you up there. But we can take you down.'

Quincy Jones

Even as a little child, I've always had that comedian kind of attitude.

Etta James

From a certain age, I sort of accepted myself for what I was. And although to other people it was like nothing ever goes right, I had a really nice attitude that I'd inherited from my parents, and especially from my dad.

Johnny Vegas

After the Meiji restoration in 1868, Japan adopted an expansionist and colonial attitude towards its neighbours. It sought to identify itself with the West and looked down upon the Asian continent as backward and inferior. For most of the next 70 years, Japan was at war, mainly with its neighbours.

Martin Jacques

The world is fortunate - for the time being, at least - that it has an American president in Obama who is prepared to take a conciliatory and concessive attitude towards America's decline and that it has a Chinese leadership which has been extremely cautious about expressing an opinion, let alone flexing its muscles.

Martin Jacques

Bob Altman had this relaxed but serious attitude. Everybody loved him. I wanted him to adopt me.

Steve Buscemi

The most important criterion is this: hire someone whose character and humility and attitude you would like to have reproduced in your church and in yourself.

John Ortberg

It remains to consider what attitude thoughtful men and Christian believers should take respecting them, and how they stand related to beliefs of another order.

Asa Gray

My attitude goes back to my childhood. I used to audition for theatrical roles, and you can't stand out in a room full of ambitious eight-year-old girls by acting the wallflower. I realised then that I couldn't do things half-heartedly.

Jessie J

I have such an extreme attitude about work, where I can just completely be derelict of my responsibilities and then when I am not derelict, I am completely indulged in it. I swing pretty wildly from the two extremes.

Geddy Lee

It got very tedious saying the same jokes in the same way with the same attitude.

Norm MacDonald

In the late '70s, maybe just before I started, there was still an attitude that if you did film you didn't do TV and vice versa, but that's gone now.

Robert Carlyle

The word 'spinster' tells you everything you need to know about our attitude of women who choose not to marry.

Caitlin Moran

Just as the left has to be more willing to question 'Government knows best,' the right has to rethink its laissez-faire attitude toward government.

Jack Kemp

Children have adopted a consumerist attitude - I dare you to entertain me.

Walter Dean Myers

Experiments with animals have long been handicapped by our anthropocentric attitude: We often test them in ways that work fine with humans but not so well with other species.

Frans de Waal

Nothing. We're all friends and friendly. So when the cameras go down, depending on the mood or the nature of the material we're dealing with, there's usually a kind of a prevailing light attitude that's floating around.

Richard Dean Anderson

Becoming an author changes your attitude too. Once you see where books come from, and how they're made, they never seem quite as sacred again.

Lev Grossman

I have very diverse tastes in music, and I don't, like, make distinctions between what I can't and can't listen to. In fact, I could never understand why anybody would do that in the first place. My attitude is, 'I can't make music if I don't like music.'

Corey Taylor

I went to the Performing Arts School and studied classical ballet. That attitude is something that's put into your head. You are never thin enough.

Carmen Electra

One by one, all of my college buddies had taken these nothing-special entry-level jobs, pushing papers for $18,000 or $21,000 a year (and hating the work besides), and I'd turn up my nose and tell them I wasn't about to get out of bed for anything less than $50,000. That was my line, my attitude.

Bill Rancic

There are a lot of movies I'd like to throw away. That's not to say that I went in with that attitude. Any film I ever started, I went in with all the hope and best intentions in the world, but some films just don't work.

Kiefer Sutherland

Nobody minded what you did in bed or what you said about God, a very civilized attitude in 1948.

Simon Raven

I always thought of myself as more American than Americans when I was living in Germany, because I always had this attitude of can-do, and if you're successful, you can show it, which is a very un-German thing, you know.

Kim Dotcom

I guess I just always had this idea that I would go to Hollywood. I had the typical 'get up and go' attitude that you have to have in order to make the brave step into the big city.

Felicia Day

I'm always excited when I make it on anyone's list - even if it's for affirmative action. My attitude is, 'Am I the token woman on this list? Because I'll take it.'

Julie Klausner

The American attitude towards efficiency and execution should always underlie architecture.

Helmut Jahn

I won't say there aren't any Harvard graduates who have never asserted a superior attitude. But they have done so to our great embarrassment and in no way represent the Harvard I know.

Derek Bok

We must advertise to U.S. business that we are there, that our attitude has changed, and that we care. When we are asked to help, we have to perform and provide the right advice.

Lawrence Eagleburger

My attitude on skis is different now. I have learned to put less pressure on myself and on the edges of my skis when I'm racing, to be keep myself more under control.

Hermann Maier

If a site is done with pleasure and a fun attitude, it's a great way to communicate with your fans.

Christopher Lambert

'UFO's' attitude toward the subject is very similar to mine. It's not an advocacy; its philosophy is more 'I want to believe this, but I want it proved.'

Dwight Schultz

The theatre only knows what it's doing next week, not like the opera, where they say: What are we going to do in five years' time? A completely different attitude.

Harrison Birtwistle

If you go on stage with the wrong attitude, or something in your performance is off, you can lose an audience in the first minute. That first minute is crucial.

Allan Carr

After the first miscarriage, I tried to take the attitude that it was my body's way of telling me that this pregnancy wasn't meant to be.

Christie Brinkley

I trained as a writer before I became a lawyer. I was headed for a life as an English professor, but that just wasn't me. I'm not a scholar; I didn't have a scholar's attitude toward literature.

Scott Turow

When I first left university, I thought about going into the private sector. But I discovered when I went to interview that I could only have a career in the back office, or doing HR. The attitude was, 'My dear lady, you cannot possibly think about going on the board.'

Pauline Neville-Jones

The Twenties have this sort of attitude where you never know what's around the corner.

Laura Carmichael

Though it may not seem like it, I never try to write about a place, per se; it's always, first and last, about story. Story is everything. Story and a bit of attitude.

Martin McDonagh

I saw 'Taxi Driver,' and 'Taxi Driver' kind of saved my life. The scene where Robert De Niro is looking at himself in the mirror saying, 'You talkin' to me? You talkin' to me? Who the hell else are you talkin' to?' That's the scene that changed my life by changing my attitude about acting.

Michael Biehn

Liberalism is a really old British tradition and it has a completely different attitude towards the individual and the relationship between the individual and the state than the collectivist response of Labour, and particularly Old Labour, does.

Nick Clegg

To me, you have to declare yourself a Chicano in order to be a Chicano. That makes a Chicano a Mexican-American with a defiant political attitude that centers on his or her right to self-definition. I'm a Chicano because I say I am.

Cheech Marin

I'm definitely attracted to other Australians; I have a laid-back attitude to life that I feel is very Australian; I love a good barbie.

Isla Fisher

The Stones are a different kind of group. I realized that when I joined them. It's not really so much their musical ability, it's just they have a certain kind of style and attitude which is unique.

Mick Taylor

Too many people say to their brokers, I can't deal with this. Take my money. Do what you want. That's the worst attitude you can have.

Maria Bartiromo

The attitude and capacity of the factory, the old metal table and the new ideas of the wooden furniture quickly and naturally suggested the possibility of metal furniture.

Donald Judd

What has happened is that to some degree they have taken an attitude where they don't listen to demos of diverse subject matters. They're looking for demos like the record the guy on the left just did.

Grandmaster Flash

When you are developing your style, you avoid weaknesses. I am not good at describing things, so I stay away from it. And if anyone is going to describe anything at all, it's going to be from the point of view of the character, because then I can use his voice, and his attitude will be revealed in the way he describes what he sees.

Elmore Leonard

I went to England in the '70s, and I was in my early 20s. There was still a residue of that era of being an underclass or colonial. I assume it must have been a more aggressive and prominent attitude 40 years before that, because Australia internationally wasn't regarded as having much cultural value. We were a country full of sheep and convicts.

Geoffrey Rush

People have often asked if I'm gay because I don't go out of my way to spit and scratch and give people attitude.

Jason Bateman

I'm quite a particular singer, and I need to feel like I can bite into the song, in a way, to make it my own. You want the challenge of the songs having some attitude.

Neneh Cherry

You can have a laugh in Los Angeles, or you can weep in Los Angeles, depending on your attitude towards it.

Miranda Richardson

I always give Lindsay so much credit for her tennis game, for her attitude, for her person, and because of how she deals with all the things. I don't think people give her enough credit for how well she's doing.

Martina Hingis

There does not seem to be that collegiality I referred to, there seems to be much more of a them versus us attitude, rather than we all have a role to play in this process so let's get on with it.

Len G. Murray

Cheney, Rumsfeld - they were Shakespearean in their attitude of impunity.

Glen Duncan

It's better for me to play with guys because Rock 'n' Roll has such an aggressive attitude.

Lita Ford

Neapolitans are extremely empathetic, whereas the typical northern attitude is more about not showing or sharing your feelings.

Toni Servillo

Bambi can't act. Bambi had major attitude.

Treat Williams

I have a real taste for doing action roles. I starred in a movie called 'Blast,' which was my first action film, and I loved the fighting - I think I've got the build, the attitude and the look for it.

Nadine Velazquez

I wasn't interested in politics. My attitude about it was, I can't make a difference no matter what I do. And the truth is, I don't even care enough to try.

Chris Jordan

It really was hand-to-mouth and you can say, 'Poor little me, how dreadful, what a deprived childhood', but I didn't feel that way at all. It's all about the attitude at home.

Carol Vorderman

I kind of resent this attitude of men that we somehow must always look good.

Sharon Gless

My feelings about my mortality are less selfish than they used to be. I used to affect a cavalier attitude to death; now I see it from my son's perspective.

Rufus Sewell

But I do think that we approach music, in of itself, with a religious attitude.

Jon Fishman

If you eat something and get fat, you should be responsible for it. I think that is the attitude of the great majority of Americans, that you should be responsible for what you eat.

Vic Snyder

I hope 'The Voice' has a fifteen-year run, don't get me wrong. But I come from nothing, and maybe it's the Irish in me, but my attitude is always like, 'They'll figure me out soon.'

Carson Daly

The directors I respect are the ones who have a collaborative attitude, who collaborate with actors.

Eric Braeden

In regard to music, I just think that it's always best to have an attitude of being a perpetual student and always look to learn something new about music, because there's always something new to learn. Don't dismiss something out of hand because you think it's either beneath you or outside of the realm of where your interests lie.

David Sanborn

I did standup for a lot of years, too, but when you come out as a standup, you get the feeling from a crowd - it's a kind of a 'make me laugh' attitude. But when you come out as an improvisor, they realize that they're suggesting everything you do. So they're already invested in the scene, and they actually want it to work.

Ryan Stiles

If you're a goal scorer, you have to have a certain attitude. I'm very serious. My missus thinks I'm a bit weird. I'm cold, I don't have many emotions. It's very rare I cry.

Michael Owen

I hate going to L.A. and dealing with the contempt people have for television and television actors. It's unbelievable the kind of attitude people take toward what is the most exciting medium we've got right now.

Michael Moriarty

I'm just part of a tradition of people who aren't pleased. I would never think anyone else who has the same attitude was getting it from me. I'd just think they're... sensible.

Jack Dee

The jokes are great but what really matters for a comedian is his performance, his whole attitude, and the laughs that he gets between the jokes rather than on top of the jokes.

Jack Dee

There were a few teachers who just did not like me because of my face. Once, I was told to stand in the corner until I cheered up. The attitude was, 'Oh, for God's sake, what's the matter with him?' But it's just a natural expression.

Jack Dee

I feel like I have as good a shot as anybody out there and I have gotten close in the past, so why not have the attitude that I can come out and play great tennis and maybe even win this tournament.

Michael Chang

I do not share the half-in, half-out attitude to the EU of some in Britain. Britain's place is in Europe.

Peter Mandelson

If you take a band like Nirvana, their biggest hits are structurally the same as even a hair metal band's biggest hits. The structure's not different - the attitude was different. Except it really wasn't. It seemed a little more human.

Buzz Osborne

Part of the whole L.A. mentality that nothing really matters unless it's a success... is such a shallow and dangerous attitude to have.

Patricia Richardson

I have an issue with others ordering for me, and I spend far too long haranguing people that my choices are the best. I apologize for the amount of conversations I have ruined with this attitude.

Ben Elliot

My father instilled in me an attitude that you couldn't really enjoy yourself unless you had done something to deserve it. So, my childhood was spent working on farms or local shops or, when I got older, in banks.

Ben Elliot

The attitude of independence toward a constructed language which all national speakers must adopt is really a great advantage, because it tends to make man see himself as the master of language instead of its obedient servant.

Edward Sapir

I broke two knuckles in my right hand when I gave Jean-Claude Van Damme an attitude adjustment. I got nothing except a medical bill.

Chuck Zito

That attitude toward women as objects may have worked for the late Sixties, but it doesn't do so now.

John Schlesinger

I go into it with the attitude that I'm not going to look at my leg, and as soon as they get the wrapping off of it, I'm like, 'I've got to look.' It's like yelling at a dog going, 'Squirrel!' I cannot not look. And then I spend the rest of the time sitting there with a wet washcloth on my forehead trying to regain consciousness.

Tony Stewart

I love Jonathan Richman - I love a lot of his music, and the thing I really like about him is his attitude. He seems very happy, and the way he performs is like, 'Don't worry, everybody, just get into it. I'm just having fun; I like when you guys are having fun.'

Mac DeMarco

There are definitely roles within this industry that are industry-related, but to be a good actor, you really have to want to act first. At the same time, my goal was never to go to Hollywood to make movies. I think if you come here with that attitude, then you've missed a few steps.

Anthony Edwards

I was never a glamour puss whose career was really based on a look or an attitude. I've been basically playing the same parts I am at 55 that I was at 35. I get cast as strong women, and that can be a mother or a judge or anything.

Jane Kaczmarek

I truly love Australia; I miss Aussie kids and their attitude!

Nicole Trunfio

I'm not concerned that my stuff isn't extreme. I don't want to be heavy. I can't think of another attitude to have toward an audience than a hopeful and a positive one. And if that includes such unfashionable things as sentimentality, well, I can afford it.

Robert Palmer

My attitude is that if anybody of any age wants to read a book, let them, but I do think that no child would want to read 'Boneland.'

Alan Garner

G.I. Joe has a heart and an attitude that feels right and familiar to me, so they could have ray guns, and they'd still feel more like real troops than many other franchises.

Karen Traviss

Gemmell's name guarantees a satisfying story and a thumping good read. I recommend all his heroic creations - 'Druss the axeman,' 'the Jerusalem man,' among others - but my favourite has to be 'Waylander': Clint Eastwood with a crossbow and the same 'Make my day, punk' attitude.

Neal Asher

Fame is O.K. I hate it, but it's O.K. I'm beginning to understand how I can be hidden. It's an attitude.

Romain Duris

I look at the NFL and see how the transition has gone at quarterback. I might be coming along at a good time. For me personally, this is about doing the same thing I've been doing at USF - just smile, have fun, enjoy the experience, keep a positive attitude and encourage my teammates. I like to feed off the people around me.

B. J. Daniels